FROM GRIEF TO GODDESS

⊱— Healing the Wounded Woman —⊰

JUDE GARRECHT

www.fromgrieftogoddess.com
www.dreamingtheseed.com

A Self-Published Title

Animal Dreaming Publishing
www.AnimalDreamingPublishing.com

From Grief to Goddess

A self-published book produced with the help and support of
ANIMAL DREAMING PUBLISHING
PO Box 5203 East Lismore NSW 2480
AUSTRALIA

Phone +61 2 6622 6147

www.AnimalDreamingPublishing.com
www.facebook.com/AnimalDreamingPublishing

First published in 2013
Copyright text © Jude Garrecht
www.FromGriefToGoddess.com
Cover art by Angie Alexandrou
Copyright cover art © Angie Alexandrou and Jude Garrecht

ISBN 978-0-9923983-0-9

This book is intended for spiritual and emotional guidance only.
It is not intended to replace medical assistance or treatment.

Designed by Animal Dreaming Publishing
Printed in Australia

Dedicated to Gaia – the ultimate Goddess in my eyes

When we insert loss and grief as an overlay to any situation we find that we are all equal in our suffering. Grief is devastating and a time consumer. It is a hard taskmaster who will not let you move on to the next stages until you have fully explored the one currently in your face. No amount of stamping your feet and saying 'enough' will help you move through it any quicker.

To think you have conquered grief before you are ready is utter denial of the process. There are layers and layers to be sifted through and healed. To bury grief is to potentially open to illness down the track. It is insidious and sneaks up on you when you least expect it. A song, a memory, a smell, a familiarity, a place, things you shared are all harsh triggers that say, "Look at me. You are not through with me yet. I am grief, name me, look at me and deal with me. What I promise you, is when you work with me rather than against me, I will make you stronger, more resilient, more open to knowing who you really are. I will help you find your personal truth; I will bring you to tears to cleanse your heart and your soul. I will bring you anger to show you how to reawaken your passion for life. I will bring you love to show you how much you are loved; I will show you just how wonderful you are. But there are no shortcuts on the healing path. I am grief and I will hold your hand and your heart. I will help you explore the depths of your feelings and raise you up once again into the light. Acknowledge me and work with me, and you will once again know joy."

These words flowed from my fingertips. A deep, meaningful dialogue from the wound called grief.

Contents

Introduction

The pain of separation took me to the pits of despair. Grief cut me like a knife in my heart.

Fourteen years we had been together and one cold winter's day, my partner packed his car and said, 'I'm leaving!'

My new journey to becoming a Goddess in my own life began the moment he uttered those words.

Post EVENT (as I now call my catalyst for personal transformation) and I discover the Goddess within me is actually alive and well. She has just been pushed down and suffocated by my feelings of unworthiness for a long, long time.

The following twelve months was a time of healing as I finally accepted that I needed to learn to love me—all of me. I lived in solitude (except for my red furry angel, Moo) in a house overlooking the wild untamed coastline. Its turbulent seas reflected my painful inner journey. I could have worn grief as a cloak of self-pity, but I chose to accept the challenge it set me, and emerge victorious as a stronger, wiser Goddess through self-discovery and examination.

From Grief to Goddess is not about judgement, however it is about *my* perceptions on how I handled my grief and became my own Goddess—a sometimes-flawed Goddess in my own eyes, but a Goddess nonetheless! I am not perfect and I do not pretend to be anything but who I am: I laugh, I cry and I laugh some more—often at myself. It is my 'realness' as a human being that I choose to share with you in *From Grief to Goddess*.

My life is unique to me! For me, it is a beautiful blend of living in a physical world with all its idiosyncrasies, challenges and adventures, coupled with my spiritually insightful experiences. It is my own unique take on the world that has helped me move through my grieving process, sometimes with grace and purpose and sometimes with a messy challenge. There have been many times that I have looked back and wondered why I wasn't lying in a crying heap more often. Don't get me wrong, there have been many tears and fears, however I have just had to cope and take my time to heal and get on with my life. I have learned a lot about who I am and it has not all been a bed of roses, but it is not all depths of despair either. It is flowing with my feelings as they surface.

We all deal with grief in our own way and this book is about my way! It is my fervent hope that *From Grief to Goddess* will help some of you who are on your own journey into grief and subsequent healing.

This book is for those who want to discover how to step into their own Goddess self!

Come on a journey with me.
This is my story.

Jude

⤴ **The Event** ⤴

June

'I have been living a lie and I hate it down here. I don't love you anymore and I haven't loved you for some time'.

My partner, whom I have loved for fourteen years, paces the slate floor as these cold harsh words spill out in a rush. I reel with the shock of this unmitigated assault. He adds, 'You want the truth, I am finally telling you the truth. I'm leaving.' His words are like physical blows to my body, my mind, my heart.

I have to sit down as I am unsteady on my feet. I am acutely aware of a new sensation building in my solar plexus. It is a knowing of truth. I know in my heart and my soul that our time together is up, that our soul contract is complete and the words he is speaking *are* in fact truth—for both of us.

I search for words and ask if it can be fixed but my feelings are overriding my thoughts and words. I *know* this as absolute truth.

He says, 'No, I don't think so,' and leaves; his parting words hit home. 'I suspect I have been holding you back anyway.' I am torn, as I hear these words as both a parting gift and an insult, an excuse for bad behaviour.

He walks out the door and I see his car driving out of our driveway for the last time.

I had not registered the reason his car was packed with his things and why he wasn't at work when I arrived home only moments ago. I had even seen his job advertised in the local paper last Saturday. When I challenged him he lied, just as he lied about everything over the fourteen years we had been together.

I loved him regardless of the lies. I always forgave him, choosing to believe my love was strong enough to overcome the pattern of lying in our relationship!

Now that he has left, I see the truth that I have been avoiding for fourteen years; the truth that it is not possible to maintain a healthy relationship when you are living a perpetual lie.

To say I am overwhelmed with grief in those initial hours is perhaps an overstatement. I am shocked yes, but not totally surprised. After all I had been in denial about the state of our relationship for many years.

I call people; friends and family and begin to fall apart.

I call him several times as he drives the four hours back to Melbourne. I ask again, 'Can it be fixed?' He answers, 'No, I don't think so.' He is still lying to me, knowing in himself that there will never be a reconciliation. He is free, and I am defeated by betrayal.

My soul knows the joy that underpins this loss, but my physical, mental, and emotional being knows only pain. And so the grieving begins.

I walk outside to stand by the inlet next to my home. The moon stretches reflectively across the inky water. The night is icy cold and hungrily feeds the cold shock inside me. I ignore the cold and sit on the earth and close my eyes, breathing in the night.

My mind drifts to the metaphoric stories I have written as a meditative journey into healing. I take a deep breath and allow my thoughts to come and go without attempting to control them. I am sitting on the earth, connecting with the moon, the water and the cool of the night. My heart rate slows, my breath is steady and I am already in a meditative state because of my grief.

My stories represent all women on their healing journey. I breathe deeply once more and soften my gaze to look into the moonlight reflected in front of me. With my inner vision and senses I become the woman in my metaphoric story.

MEDITATION
Reflection

The silvery glow of the moon reflects on the surface of the gently rippling water. I step from the shadows on the banks of the river and into the languid coolness.

Naked, I float on my back as I bare my body and my soul to Grandmother Moon, offering up my wounded woman to be healed on this wondrous night.

My shadow emerges from the depths of the deep, cool river and begins to dance evocatively over the surface of the reflective water. The watery depths offer no fear now as my shadow taunts me with its deceptive ways and harsh judgements, daring me to accept Shadow back into my life.

Fear and judgement are no longer present as I willingly open my vulnerable self to the healing power of this full moon. I quietly acknowledge my own glorious imperfections and personal truths as a necessary part of my journey.

I float silently, waiting for the right moment in which to merge with my shadow self.

I am ready to become whole in every part of my being. I am ready to heal old wounds. Grandmother Moon rises high in the sky until she is directly overhead, her light shining into my womb. Shadow notices the glow and stops dancing. She is curious about this new light.

Shadow moves closer to my floating form. The closer Shadow draws, the brighter this light shines. Shadow feels the pull of the light and desperately wants to be a part of it as it shines within me. Shadow is tired of dancing alone. She has a lot to teach me about freedom of the spirit and how to dance evocatively in the moonlight.

Grandmother Moon begins her slow descent and her healing light moves back to the reflective water. Shadow has to move quickly or miss her chance to become one with me again. She *wants*, she *needs* to be a part of me again.

I close my eyes and quietly invite Shadow to merge with me, to be a part of my whole being again.

Shadow slips into me effortlessly and I feel my wholeness. The healing from Grandmother Moon is complete.

I emerge from the water and stand resplendent and glowing in my nakedness. I thank Grandmother Moon and the river for encouraging my shadow to once again be a part of my journey to wholeness.

ᐁ— AFFIRMATIONS INSPIRED BY MEDITATIONS —ᐃ

Embrace the healing power of the full moon/
heal old wounds/
dance your way to wholeness/
embrace your light/
accept your shadow

Chapter Two

❧ It's Early Days ❧

June

Immense sadness overwhelms me and threatens to swamp me. The tears flow effortlessly as I mourn the end of my relationship.

I wake this morning from a restless sleep and realise I am alone in my bed. I reach out my hand and I can only feel the cold emptiness beside me.

Shell shocked by the previous day's events, I am nauseous and unable to eat, left wondering how this could have happened. His actions and words are still stinging my wounded self.

Friends and family call to check on me. I am many hours' drive from most of them and I know I have so much support, even if it is at the end of the phone. I talk over and over what is in my heart. I answer questions and guess at the answers. I am fine, I am sad, I am in shock, I am grieving and I am lonely.

My red furry angel, Moo, is my constant companion; she is love on four legs. I adopted Moo in the months prior to the EVENT and I am grateful that she is with me now. She looks at me with big brown sad eyes and leans gently against me. I sob into her fur and she stays close.

How do I move through those early days of grief? One moment at a time, that's how! Sometimes it is microseconds when coping with grief.

The ocean, the light-filled sunrise and rich colours of the setting sun become my lifelines. Meditation is easy in the depths of my grief. There is just me now and these small shards of light filled moments give me hope.

In my heart I have long known this time would come and I feared the feelings it would evoke. Grief didn't disappoint. It lived up to all my night terrors and fears.

MEDITATION
Crystalline Synergy

Just before sunrise, I place my clear crystal upon the sand, setting it amongst the ripples created by the previous night's winds. Even the harshest of winds creates a shifting and ever-changing beauty; the constant flow of life is change.

The crystal is positioned between me and the direction of the sun in order to harness its power as soon as it rises regally in the east.

Within minutes the sun peaks over the horizon. I begin to feel the magnetic pull of the crystal upon the sun and the sun upon the crystal. This same pull is felt deep within my womb. My creative inner light is working in collaboration with sun and crystal.

The intense vibration of the three forces of sun, crystal, and womb pulling at each other's field of energy builds to a crescendo of pure light and love. A wave of climactic ecstasy washes over me and I am replete.

ᖫ— AFFIRMATIONS INSPIRED BY MEDITATIONS —ᖫ

Heal your womb/
love your ever-changing beauty/
embrace love/
create your own ecstasy/
welcome your creative light/
initiate shifts

Chapter Three

☙ I am Single ☙

June

I go to The Well (a sacred place of mine that is next to the Southern Ocean) with the intention of energetically releasing us both in whatever form that may be—to be together or apart for our highest good. I sob; I am so sad. I make a wish for happiness, joy and love for us both—together or apart.

Three days have passed and I register that I am newly single. I make some initial decisions. I will move house to a bigger town. This house fills me with grief over the hopes and dreams that are now shattered. Returning to study is a much-needed goal. It will allow me breathing space whilst I pull my life together. I decide to become vegetarian. I join Weightwatchers to shed unhealthy kilos. I walk my dog to become physically fit. I need some tangible goals to work towards, to keep me putting one foot in front of the other, to give me hope for a brighter future.

The decisions I am making are mine alone. There is no more 'we' in decision making and I am scared. There is no 'back me up' if I get it wrong. It is just me!

Sadness is a constant. It stays with me like an unwelcome stranger in my home. It assaults me in my every waking moment. Do I really think I can just get on with my life and not plunge headlong into grief? Reality check here girl, you are human and humans suffer as they learn how to heal a deeply wounded heart.

Nausea resulting from the feelings of betrayal erupts from deep within me like a volcano spewing lava on some low-lying village. The pattern of lies that I accepted and forgave over many years has culminated in this one major life EVENT.

The Well offers me time for inner reflection. I sit on the sand at the edge of the cliff overlooking the Southern Ocean. I reflect on my family and friends who are supporting me in my decisions and nurturing me as I navigate my way through the early days of grief.

I take three deep breaths and listen to the sounds of the waves crashing onto the cliffs below. The cold wind blows around me as I hunker down deep inside my jacket. I breathe in the aroma of the pungent sea.

Grief takes me immediately into a meditative state. The meditation I am about to do reminds me that healing in community rather than in isolation is an important step on the path through grief to wholeness. My women friends have gathered around me in recent days as a sisterhood of support.

I feel their support around me now as I sit on my cliff top.

MEDITATION
Secret Women's Business

The women gather together for secret women's business—to sit in sacred circle. They come from all over the Universe as they are called by one of their own; a wounded woman ready to heal.

The women are veiled to preserve the sanctity of my inner healing journey. Their feminine presence alone will bring the supportive vibration of the collective sisterhood.

This is secret women's business—a personal healing journey.

The women come together for storytelling and healing.

I sit quietly in the centre of the sisterhood's sacred circle. My painful story stirs deep within me, bubbling to the surface to be spoken. I am ready to heal my story and so begins the telling of it one last time.

When my story is shared and healed in this inner realm, I return my consciousness to the cliff top overlooking the ocean. I feel peace in the knowing that I am well supported by my sisterhood of friends.

❧— AFFIRMATIONS INSPIRED BY MEDITATIONS —❧

You are healing/
embrace your Divine Feminine/
find your supportive sisterhood/
sit in sacred circle and be still

Chapter Four

❧ **Signs of Hope** ❧

July

I had been in total denial about the toxicity of our relationship. I now realise that our relationship was toxic for some time. I just didn't realise it whilst living in it. I held on too tight; he didn't hold on tight enough, and we didn't see it or maybe didn't want to see it.

The wind blows viciously as it whips the sandy beach around me. Mammoth waves pound the coast, the sound deafening.

My troubled mind formulates a plan to win him back on *any* terms. 'I want him back!' I shout into the wind. The fierceness of the wind flings my words back to me. My heart flickers with that inner knowing that he isn't coming back. I release my words to the wind and I am silent, for now.

I quietly ask for a 'sign'; a message from life to let me know that I will come through this intense pain. I look to the horizon and see a magnificent vibrant rainbow. This is the only sign I need for now. I know I will heal in the course of time.

Rainbows are a powerful and positive symbol for me in times of transformation. Symbols are the language of the soul and my soul has just spoken to me loud and clear. You will prevail; keep going.

MEDITATION
Cloak of Colour

The rain clears and I venture outside to witness the cleansing nature of water on earth. My world has been washed clean.

The rain begins to fall again and a watery sunlight filters through the heavy droplets.

I stand in the rain, loving the feel of the water as it runs in rivulets down my body. I close my eyes and sigh at the glory of being washed as clean as the earth.

When I open my eyes I see a cloak of colour enveloping my naked form. A rainbow has draped itself around my shoulders before falling to the ground in folds of concentrated light.

I close my eyes once more to feel each colour in its purity. Wholeness pervades my being. I centre myself and connect fully with my world through this rainbow light.

☙ AFFIRMATIONS INSPIRED BY MEDITATIONS ❧

**Stand proud in your nakedness/
dance in the rain/
drape your body with rainbow colours/
embrace your inner light/
connect with the natural world**

Chapter Five

❧ One Step at a Time ❧

July

The initial shock of his lies has worn off and I only have love and the feeling of loss of losing him. The greater part of me, my soul, is showing me that I am ready to fly. There is excitement fluttering within me. I feel that he has set us both free to move on to the next phase of our lives. Today I feel strong and powerful.

Sitting quietly on the lounge room floor in meditation, I see my old life completely destroyed by wildfire. My eyes suddenly open in surprise because I am not sure I am ready to be relieved of my old life just yet. I also see a new man in my future but it is far too soon to be seeing more into this than hope and potential. '*You are a beautiful woman,*' I hear, '*in every way.*' I am not sure yet that I won't fight to regain what I am so desperately missing but this snippet of hope for a brighter future bubbles gently away under the surface of my psyche.

I understand that I am loved when I allow myself to listen to my soul in those quiet moments of solitude.

The wheels of my new goals are now in motion. Survival is my ultimate goal at this moment, however practicality seeps into my consciousness. I look for a new property to rent. I book my counselling course. I become vegetarian and I follow the Weightwatchers plan to move into good health.

One small step at a time, Jude, one small step. There is a Divine order to my life and I cannot seem to queue-jump to the goals I would like to see happen first. I am in no condition to fight against the Divine order of my new life. It must unfold naturally and in the right sequence at the optimum time. This is the new way of being for me. No more multi-tasking! Assimilate one goal at a time and then the next one begins to evolve.

I am only five days into the grieving process and I think I am in a recovery phase. I am strong, I have made plans, I am woman, hear me roar! All that denial—ah, the glory of denial. For now though, my inner strength is encouraging me to set tangible goals.

My goals are achievable and the wheels are now in constant motion, albeit slowly. I *am* surviving and perhaps becoming a little excited about my future.

It's decision time! Live life like there is no tomorrow; have fun and take no prisoners. Okay, so that last bit's a joke. But I am no longer a prisoner in my own mind. I am free! I have no idea how this fun 'thing' is going to manifest, however it's a good plan.

Something has changed; shifted and I like it. The blinkers of my old life have been removed from my eyes. Bring it on, I say!

My meditations bring me to a place of healing and peace. I love it.

MEDITATION
Hidden Beauty

I wake from a deep, dreamless sleep. As I focus my eyes, I can see magnificent cloud formations embracing my beloved mountains, temporarily hiding them from view.

A smile plays on my lips as I ready myself to uncover the gift, the beauty I know is veiled within the embrace.

I know that like the mountains, our beauty is sometimes hiding beneath a cloudy embrace. Clouds eventually lift to reveal the inner beauty that is *always* present.

I need patience and I call on my innate wisdom to help me understand that my personal inner cloud will soon lift to reveal essential keys to unlock my healing journey.

I emerge from my meditation with renewed hope in my heart. Patience is my clear message. The wisdom gleaned in my meditation shows me my inner journeying is guiding me well and I must trust the grieving process.

∽— AFFIRMATIONS INSPIRED BY MEDITATIONS —✑

**Embark on an inner journey/
remember your inner gifts/
reveal your true beauty/
be patient/ tap into your innate wisdom**

Chapter Six

❧ **Revelations** ☙

July

My heart is quiet, loving and supporting me on my new journey.

Making sense of my life when the dreams and goals we enjoyed as a couple have flown out the window is a continual challenge. Walking to my sacred place at the edge of the world becomes a daily occurrence; a chance to reflect on my grief and the powerful journey ahead. The wild, untamed coastline offers solace to my broken heart. The intensity of the sound of the ocean peels away more layers of grief, rewarding me with clarity in mind and heart.

I have experienced three major intimate relationships in life. In an attempt to understand the inherent lessons in these relationships and the part I played in them, I sit quietly on the cold cliff top and wait for the wisdom to come. The cold winter wind numbs my face; tears sting my eyes making it hard to see the ocean in front of me. I close my eyes and allow my mind to search the deep recesses of my memories.

Perhaps a glimmer of understanding will prevent a recurrence in any potential new relationship. I meditate to see the bigger picture of my life.

I married for the first time at the tender age of nineteen. Control, jealousy, and violence were the lessons in this relationship. At the time I thought I deserved his ill treatment. It is with the benefit of many years of personal growth that I finally understand why women stay in unhealthy relationships. There is a constant thought that you have no choice. I was told that I had made my bed by marrying him and now I had to lie in it. Five years later, he left and I soared like an eagle into my next relationship just six weeks later.

I married for the second time and learned the lessons of love and pain.

Thirteen years and two children later, I was the one who left. The financial and emotional pain, as well as the physical upheaval, left a path of devastation in its wake for both of us. Hindsight tells me I didn't think I deserved great love.

Lies, secrets and deceit were the foundations of my third relationship. The wounding lessons of a one sided relationship and ongoing emotional detachment were a constant source of pain. The end of our sacred contract was an intense and heartbreaking experience. When it's 'time's up' in a relationship, life becomes a double-edged sword. There is the suffering that comes with being human and living with grief, and the wisdom that the relationship has reached an abrupt but natural conclusion.

Leaving me was the final gift as I had not yet learned the lesson of letting go when something does not serve me well.

The relationships I have experienced so far in my life have been steep learning curves as I understand the patterns of my personal belief systems surrounding them. Feeling unworthy of great love in a relationship has been my lifelong belief. Ouch! It hurts to be real and take responsibility for my part in these relationships breaking down.

The stories that surface to be examined can be very 'in your face' or conversely sneak up on you when you are not looking. This one was an 'in-my-face, kick-me-in-the-gut, I-get-it' type of story.

Peace settles within me as I recognise the role I played in these chapters.

My connection with the cliff top and the turbulent seas restores equilibrium in my mind, body, soul, and emotions. A song erupts from within me. A sacred Aboriginal song about earth connection, taught to me by my mentor and friend, Minmia, Aboriginal senior woman of the Wirradjirri people. It fills me with joy and a measure of peace. I sing loudly to the ocean, feeling its power deep within my core. Gratitude to my natural surroundings for their healing gift wells in my throat. I have begun to heal this chapter in my life.

MEDITATION
Emotional Cleansing

The tree stands as a sentinel in the centre of the lake, its leafy reflection a mirror image to its majestic beauty. I stand silently on the grassy bank at the edge of the lake that is home to the tree.

I feel a gentle pull within me; an intuitive expression that beckons me to swim out to the tree, my inner turmoil opening me to the lure of the trees vibration. Its golden light glows from deep within its gnarled trunk; light that reaches far beyond its leaf laden branches.

My emotions reach into the dark night of my soul. I have nothing left to give, nothing left to express. My inner light is dimmed with the tumultuous events that are currently shaping my journey.

The water laps at my feet and I feel encouraged to immerse myself into the bracing coolness. I surrender my pain and emotions to the watery depths of the lake and the pull of the sentinel tree, stoic in its watery surrounds. I slowly lower myself into the water and begin to swim, stroke-by-stroke, out to the tree.

Water, as a representation of emotions envelopes me with a loving embrace, encouraging me to keep going, to keep moving toward the healing light. The closer I swim toward the light-filled tree, the more I realise that I am winning the challenge to heal my deep emotional wounds.

I reach the tree and climb into the welcoming branches. The light from the trunk of the tree embraces me and fills me with immense peace and harmony. I know I will heal my old wounds. My healing journey has *already* begun. I feel safe and loved as I nestle further into the light filled branches, spending time in much-needed solitude before I return to my outer life to complete this healing cycle.

ᥒ— AFFIRMATIONS INSPIRED BY MEDITATIONS —ᥫ

Awaken your intuition/
connect with your inner light/
immerse yourself in positive feelings/
surrender your pain/
welcome peace and harmony

Chapter Seven

❧ **What was I Thinking?** ❧

July

He is coming on Sunday to pick up the rest of his things. I will make him lunch so we part on good terms.

There are many times when I feel I want him back. Profound dreams usually follow that yell, *'What are you thinking? Are you mad?'* Not that he has indicated that he will be back. It is all my own imagination and wishful thinking. Ongoing betrayal is the fodder of my dreams and as a result I plunge into grief once more.

He is coming to collect more of his things and I want to make lunch? Clearly I am not thinking straight. Am I hoping he will see what he is missing out on? Run into my arms and say he has made a mistake? Make love to me, see the new improved me? Mind is overruling soul.

He arrives and I try my best to be upbeat. I miss him; I miss his arms around me. My soul is reminding me of his lying and secretive ways that saw the end of our relationship, however I am adept in ignoring the messages. I want to be noticed as a desirable woman. I have not been acknowledged this way in a long time. Why do I think he will start now? Why do I think I can have crumbs for a relationship and be okay with that?

My self esteem plummets once more. I want to feel his arms around me. I want him to say he loves me. A fantasy I have conjured up for myself. It is never going to happen but I hold out hope. We are comfortable in each other's company once more. Confusion sits like a stone in my heart.

His car is full to overflowing. We hug and I cry. I so don't want to cry. It gives him power I think. I am weak and he is free. He leaves, again, and I fall apart and grieve some more. How much more can I take? The pain of the secondary loss is felt like a crushing blow in my heart.

I am told that there are worse things in the world than separation but my pain is not measured by outside events. It is mine alone to own. Outwardly I show a confident woman, inwardly my pain is deep. I am out of balance with life. Retreating from the world for a time to meditate brings me back into a state of balance between my masculine and feminine selves.

MEDITATION
Twin Flames

The forest is quiet, the carpet of needles masking my footfalls as I approach the giant redwoods.

A sharp intake of breath from me is the only discernible sound in this private sanctuary as I reach the sacred tree of twin flames. Excitement fills the air; tangible, real.

I circle the base of the tree, its gnarled body splitting into two trunks just above the burl. Each trunk reaches skyward, side by side, individual but part of the same original seed.

I reach out and place my hand on one of the huge twin trunks. I notice a masculine hand reaching around the opposite trunk. I step forward; so too does Man. Nothing is spoken; twin flames meet and there is no need for verbal expression.

We climb the tree to sit together in the fork of its bulky base, where one tree becomes two. I rest my head on his shoulder; he wraps his arms protectively around me. We sit side-by-side in perfect harmony, twin souls, masculine and feminine, complete in our wholeness.

Note: Each flame, each aspect of Woman and Man is unique as they travel their own journey through life. The beginning of time separated them to learn about individuality whilst understanding their journey together, in the perfect balance of wholeness as both feminine and masculine. This meditation can also represent the coming together of our own masculine and feminine in perfect balance.

ᴄᴅ AFFIRMATIONS INSPIRED BY MEDITATIONS ᴄᴅ

Awaken the sacred flame within/
listen with your heart/
know that you are whole and complete/
embrace your individuality/

Chapter Eight

❧ I need Answers ❧

August

We had fourteen years together. In my opinion, the experience of being together was a true soul connection. There was a lot of learning from each other. It seems now though we have journeyed as far as we can as a couple.

Fourteen long years together and I need answers. Alone in my grief, I scream out to him, 'What went wrong? Why did you leave? Why did you begin a relationship with me?' I deserve some measure of understanding.

I am spent, physically, emotionally and mentally. There are days when all feels right in my world and then for some inexplicable reason I wake from my slumber and feel the depths of despair as I plunge deep into my grief once more. I sob to myself 'How much more pain can I take?' 'This is only the end of a relationship,' I tell myself 'no one died.' It doesn't help.

It is in reality only six weeks since the EVENT and I feel I should be over it? Get a grip girl. Spiritually I know the rightness of separation; my human self says feel the pain of loss.

'Our time together was enjoyable,' he says when I am finally able to reach him. 'I loved you as much as I could love anyone. I just need to be on my own.'

My inner truth filter says he is finally telling me the truth. I get it, I finally get it. Denial has been my friend and ally for so many years and now my awareness of truth is like escaping from a dark hole in the ground.

'Why did you begin a relationship with me?' I ask. 'You are a nice person,' he replies 'and I wanted the experience of being in a relationship.'

Anger refuses to rise to the surface of my conscious mind at his remarks. He used me for his experience but, after all, it was my experience as well.

Sharing my story with someone who will listen without interruption or advice is my current goal. In my heart I feel the ocean call to me with its rough, wind-battered cliff waiting patiently at the water's edge. I know just the place to sit and share this emerging story.

MEDITATION
Grandfather Rock

Grandfather Rock is my favourite place to visit.

It is a place where I feel safe and nurtured as I lean against his craggy features.

When I feel the need to escape the world for a while or want someone to listen to my painful stories without interruption or when I crave inspiration from a loving guide, I seek out Grandfather Rock.

His patience is endless, his presence healing. Grandfather Rock has stood as a sentinel of healing since the beginning of time.

He speaks no words, has no arms to wrap around me and yet his quiet countenance is supporting my every need.

Today, as I rest my body against him, I am instantly aware of his powerful presence.

An old and deeply personal story wells up from within me. I begin to talk. Grandfather Rock listens and the next healing cycle has begun.

⮜— AFFIRMATIONS INSPIRED BY MEDITATIONS —⮞

Trust that you are safe/
share your story/
seek inspiration from nature/
trust your inner guidance/
speak your truth

Chapter Nine

∾ A Strong Mind is not ∾ my Friend

August

'I want him back!' This is my first thought as I wake this morning. Dammit, where did that come from?

A plan formulates in my feverish mind. I want to travel Australia with him. I can study whilst travelling. I want to keep on loving him and have him love me. Adventure can be our glue that holds us together. My mind says this will work.

Excitement builds. I am so sure he will say *'Yes, let's do it!'* that I push all semblance of reality out the door. In my heart of hearts I know I am setting myself up for a fall and yet the thoughts don't stop. I am prepared to do anything to make this dream (or is it a nightmare?) come true. All on his terms of course. The seed of our new way of life just needs to be planted with him.

A strong mind is not my friend. Irrational thoughts conjure up all manner of manipulating ways that will be to my advantage. The truth is, manipulation and scheming to get what I want only sets me up for a monumentous fall.

I make a whole ritual out of my manipulative ways. I have yet to realise that I am manipulating my situation in order to release the pain of my grief. What he wants is not even on my radar.

Writing a letter, saying prayers of hope for a positive outcome in my favour and going to my favourite place at The Well are all spoiled ingredients for my growing desperation.

My heart is full of love once more or what I think is love. This will work,

I know it will work, please let it work, I pray. My letter floats on the wind into the ocean and I am alive with hope.

Denial of the voice of my soul, who tells me that I will be plunged once more into grief, is the equivalent of placing my fingers in my ears to drown out the sound of a parent offering advice. 'I don't want to listen,' I yell.

Our relationship has had hiccups (this is what I am calling the lies and secretiveness at this time) however we were really good together. Where does this fantasy come from? Do I really have rose-tinted glasses on again? 'Go away inner voice of reason,' I counter. 'I have no need of your guidance. You only cause me pain and suffering.'

'We will be better partners now as a result of our time apart,' I justify. I have a very vivid and creative imagination and it is firing on all cylinders. I have all the answers to our problems and we can overcome anything!

Who am I kidding? Planning and scheming is intense and finally I am satisfied everything is in place and all he needs to say is, yes, of course I will do this with you.

I am about to fall hard—again. My heart is tapping on my consciousness so loud that I cannot ignore her any longer. There is a quiver of anxiety welling from deep within me. My head though, keeps ploughing ahead, determined to see this plan through to the end and stuff the consequences.

The clock shows 4:40am as I open my eyes and blink blearily at it. Realisation hits me like a sledge hammer. Travelling with him is not an option. I will be settling for a journey that may only last a few years—if he agrees that is.

Family, friends and my new career would be a lifetime away. The revelations keep coming. He can never give me the love I deserve.

My body aches from head to toe with inflammation. A migraine grips me like a vice. My body is truly my barometer. I am not going anywhere, anytime soon.

The rug of manipulation has been pulled out from under me and I have fallen in a heap of body-numbing pain. My intuition is telling me that I am well supported. The highs and lows of separation and subsequent manipulation may not have been so prevalent if I had trusted that inner voice from the beginning. A strong mind is not always my best friend.

I am abandoned and my dreams have been unceremoniously ripped away from me, even if at this time it is only in my own mind. The challenges keep coming and I ride the tides of change like a seasoned board rider. Sometimes I ride the crest and sometimes I am pulled under by the swell.

MEDITATION
Survival

The grey-coloured waves crash on the shore, foaming and angry. I drag myself from the sea before it claims me as its unwilling bride. Raw emotion spills from me in alternating screams of anguish and pain and tears of joy at my survival.

As I lay upon the damp sand, I know I have been damaged by the rough hands of the sea. Tossed about like a rag doll, the sea's plaything, until I finally surrender my pain to a greater power. No longer at the mercy of the oppressive sea, I am discarded.

My inner torment is excruciating, my physical body already repairing itself. I need to heal my *inner* pain.

I am victorious in my survival. I drag myself to a small opening in the rocks just above the shoreline. I am safe once more.

I sleep awhile until a bright light rouses me from my healing rest. Carved into the side of the rocky opening is a small window in the shape of a dove, a dove of peace that shines intensely within this natural sanctuary. Its light fills this tiny cavern and falls over me as a blanket of pure healing light.

I am healed! I am victorious! I have fought for my survival, surrendered my pain and won!

࢙— AFFIRMATIONS INSPIRED BY MEDITATIONS —࢙

**Express your joy/
allow the tears to flow/
rest, it's essential right now/
find solace in the natural world**

Chapter Ten

⌁ **What do I want?** ⌁

September

My daydreams are now peppered with the qualities I want in a new man. It reads like a shopping list. Where would I shop for these ingredients? I wonder sceptically. Truthful, loving, affectionate, romantic, spiritual, love me deeply, laugh and did I mention truthful? Do they really exist as an embodiment of one person? I question. I am sure they must! This mental shopping list includes everything I have not experienced in the past.

Great love is the feast of my fantasies. Healing is well and truly underway and I have been on my own for a few months. I must be ready to dive into the waters of love again, right?

I crave love! Loving arms to embrace me and keep me safe and warm. I want to feel desired, to be told I am beautiful and worthwhile. I yearn for love to knock on my door.

No one comes knocking just yet. Healing my grief is not over. There are days when I can conquer the world and other days I dive headlong into the well of pain that separation creates. When I dive, I dive deep. Often, I feel I am drowning in grief. Emotional exhaustion is taking a physical toll on my wellbeing.

Guilt is a constant as I see others just getting on with life. Shoulders back, chin up and carry on! After all, my mind says, it's just a separation. No one has died. That accusation rears its ugly head often as time marches forward.

I wake feeling nauseous and anxious – again. Decisions I have made seem frozen in time as I lurch unwillingly into a new round of grief. The weight of making my own decisions without the safety net of having a backup is overwhelming. I have to be the responsible grownup and make decisions that are just for me. It is exciting and anxiety inducing all at the same time. Contradiction seems to be my middle name.

Walking my talk is my challenge or should I say mission, should I choose to accept it. It is time to take up the reigns of my life and become all I want it to be. Success is as fearful as failure to me. I don't yet know what success looks like. There is no backup plan in my partner should everything fall in a messy heap. Perhaps this is what I really wanted when I created a shopping list of qualities in a man; a support person to be there for me just in case.

Grief is not done with me yet. Sadness sits like a stone in my heart once more. My tank of life-force energy and joy appears to have run dry. My personal happiness was clearly not based on truth.

Memories surface and I think I am still very much in love. Poetry I have written for him in our earlier life together, a loving photo, a letter of love he wrote to me, remembering that we had a telepathic connection, all feed my sadness. How could things have changed so much?

Working on acceptance, forgiveness and trust for my future are my life lines to healing.

I ache for his arms around me. I miss him with every fibre of my being but I struggle to understand why I still want him back when there is a history of lies. There will be no reconciliation anyway. He has made that abundantly clear. Sobbing hard, my heart aches once more with the pain of grief.

The vast expanse of ocean where I live is my sanctuary in times of intense grief. I flee to the cliff top overlooking the vibrant aquamarine seas to find solace in the sound of the pounding waves.

My surroundings lure me into a meditative state. I breathe deeply of the pungent sea air and close my eyes for a moment. My heart rate slows and my breath becomes steady once more.

Under the heartache I sense an awakening of a glimmer of hope. Shining through the grief, I hold onto the belief that life is about to get a whole lot brighter. When I shift the negative, I see clearly that I alone am in charge of my life. Life is about putting one foot in front of the other. That is all I am capable of for now.

For the first time in many months I smile at my potential future. It is a little scary stepping out on my own but watch out world, this Goddess in the making is ready to roll.

MEDITATION
Water Wears Away Stone

I stop to cup the water in my hands from the pool below the gentle waterfall. The slow trickle of cool water on the worn stones creates a mesmerising effect.

I sit by the pool and listen to the rhythmic plop as the water strikes each stone on its way down to the pool below.

My heart rate slows and my breathing becomes shallow as I slip further and further into the hypnotic sensations that water on stone creates.

I trail my fingers over the surface of the water, creating ripples that reach the outer edges of the pool.

The change in vibration created by the ripples soon impacts on me. My still form begins to sway with the musical accompaniment.

I stand and begin to dance, feeling the free form of my movements deep within my womb.

Within this dance of ecstasy I hear 'Water Wears Away Stone'. I understand the message clearly: when a wounded woman feels pain and suffering within her, it is the gradual healing that the free-flowing forms of nature provides that will ultimately wear away the hurt.

The dance of healing is a gentle journey.

∾— AFFIRMATIONS INSPIRED BY MEDITATIONS —↷

**Move your body in harmony with the sounds of nature/
dance in ecstasy/
change the look and feel of your environment/
be gentle on yourself**

Chapter Eleven

❧ Dreaming the Answers ❧

September

My nighttimes are busy with powerful messages for my journey. Any lingering thoughts or affection toward him provoke intense dreams, usually about betrayal.

Dreams are the language of the soul and my soul is speaking to me, loud and clear. It doesn't want me entertaining any loving expressions toward a man who betrayed me with lies and secrets.

When we first arrived in our new home, I dreamed of a huge, black snake. I knew what it meant, but I was again in denial. After all we had not long moved to this new place and everything seemed rosy on the surface of our life together.

The message from the snake meant big change was coming and that it involved him. There was no indication of the content of the change, just that the size of the change was BIG! Snakes shed their skin; shedding the old ways in order to grow into the new.

Other dreams post-EVENT involved him being uncommunicative or unresponsive and holding me back from being involved with my potential new life. Each time I felt any benevolence toward him, I would immediately dream the reality of what being with him again would be like.

It is still a fantasy I hold on to that one day we might reconcile. In my heart I know this will never happen.

Personal experience has taught me that deep grief can block intuition and it is often only in our dreams that soul can truly enlighten us and shine a light on the journey ahead.

I have one last dream in the house we have lived as a couple. I am single and about to embark on a trip on a bus with other singles. Waking from this dream in a state of joy is a relief as I have finally received a message that I am free of him.

MEDITATION
Turbulence

The earth beneath my feet feels warm and soft. I tread mindfully, wanting to be fully present in each step as I make my way through the scrubby bush.

As I walk, I hear a low moan coming to me on the gentle winds. I stop to listen. My senses are now alert to the insistent voice of the wind.

Wind begins to increase her strength, the moan a little louder. I feel a stirring of my own senses. I feel the presence of a turbulent energy.

The eerie moan is more distinctive now. Words begin to form within the breath of the wind.

Wind stirs the red earth into a funnel of sand in order to become visible to me. My senses heighten, I hear, *'The message I bring to you today is one of feeling your inner turbulence. This turbulence is a gift of discernment, to know the difference between what is of benefit for you and your journey, and what to discard. Trust your inner voice that guides you so well.'*

The wind becomes silent and the funnel of sand drops to the earth.

I take another step forward on the warm, soft earth. My senses are fully awakened now to the discernment of my own inner voice.

ᕲ— AFFIRMATIONS INSPIRED BY MEDITATIONS —ᕲ

**Pay attention to your inner voice/
tread mindfully through life/
be fully present/
look to the messages offered by nature**

Chapter Twelve

∼ **On the Move – Again!** ∼

September

Okay, Universe, here is my list of wants for my new home: Can you please provide me with a house with great views over the ocean, a fenced yard for my red furry angel, two storeys, three bedrooms, great kitchen and bathroom and at a rent I can afford. I know this is a tall order for a home overlooking the ocean but there is no doubt in my mind that my call will be answered.

Within a matter of days I find my dream home. The owner is obliging and agrees to every one of my wants including the amount of rent I want to pay, length of lease and no bond. Uninterrupted views of the ocean from my upstairs lounge room and balcony, with its spectacular sunsets, are the ultimate sealer in this negotiation. Another goal achieved.

Anger surfaces like another volcanic eruption on the day I move house. Memories of bitter sweet moments emerge as I move my belongings to a new abode. I am aggrieved that I have to organise everything and move on my own this time. There are still so many of his belongings amongst my personal treasures and he is not here to move them with me.

My relocating angels arrived this morning in the form of my sons but now they are gone and I am alone. Doubling over with the pain of renewed grief, it hits me that I am indeed alone with no one to share in this sanctuary of beauty. Life sucks, I think as I crawl fully clothed into my bed! Pulling my knees up to my chest I sob into my pillow as my red furry angel watches on with sad, knowing eyes.

Gratitude for her and my new home should make me happy. Loneliness is my only companion tonight. As I drift off into a dreamless sleep I recall a meditation and softly call to my power animals to guard me and take away my pain. I am spent, I need help.

The anger dissipates as quickly as it came. A new dawn has arrived.

Three months have passed since the EVENT and I am standing on my balcony overlooking the bush and the Southern Ocean. Like a cat I stretch my body and bask in the blue-skied, sun-drenched spring day.

Sea Eagle glides effortlessly over the treetops and the water. Mesmerised, I feel her energetic presence inside of me. My eyes are glued to her dipping and weaving over the trees. My breath and my heart rate slow. I enter a meditative state with my eyes open. Suddenly, I am gliding with her. I am her. I am winging my way on the breeze as I lock my eyes onto my target. I am free spirited. I am free to be me.

Acknowledging her message, I understand that I must glide just above whatever I am working on and seize opportunities as they appear. No need to soar to great heights for now. That will come later. Bless you, Sea Eagle.

I thrive on my study workload. A new home and a new calling are my solid foundations when life feels anything but stable at times. The goals I seeded in my initial grief are beginning to germinate and take form. I am content.

I have never lived on my own for this length of time. Three months and I am really starting to enjoy myself. I am healing—not just from this separation but from other relationships as well.

MEDITATION
Power Broker

I stand gazing at the setting sun. I contemplate the meaning of the coming darkness as the sun sinks slowly behind the tree tops.

With the onset of night, my old fears arise. The long night ahead will offer no comfort to a fearful womb.

In its final moments, the last vestiges of its light expand and its rays fill the surrounding space with an illuminated presence.

I note a totemic animal within the cloudy sunset.

The appearance of Jaguar, with a light-filled chest, awakens the primal woman within my own womb.

I roar softly to myself, acknowledging my innermost power.

It is within the power of my inner animal that I find the strength to heal old wounds. Jaguar speaks to me and asks me to remember my primordial power—the power to heal the darkness within and thus live my extraordinary life without interference from old fears.

☙— AFFIRMATIONS INSPIRED BY MEDITATIONS —☙

Expand your horizons/
awaken the primal feminine energy within you/
acknowledge your primordial power/
you are stronger than you think/
your inner darkness is healed

Chapter Thirteen

❧ **Emerging Goddess** ☙

October

There are more good days than crappy days. I am learning to laugh again. A wonderful support network of family and friends is the catalyst for healing my grief. I have been adopted by my wonderful local community and I soon realise that one cannot heal in isolation. I need the support of my community.

It is from this safe, nurturing environment that I discover the things I missed out on in my relationship are all around me. Truth, love, appreciation, and affection are here in abundance. I am very blessed. I am once more in love with life!

There are times when I also need my solitude. My home has become my sanctuary where I retreat from the world to heal another layer of grief when it arises. Watching the ever-changing colours as the sun sets each evening puts me into a contemplative mood. I first imagine the setting sun taking my grief and wrapping it in a red, orange and gold blanket of pure love and healing.

With the last vision of the sun setting on the horizon, my final image is that the vibrant colours represent a dragon breathing fire as she takes my grief down into the emotional watery realms of healing. Fire and water cleanse my hurting soul.

Tomorrow is a new day. With the rising sun I will embrace the joy of new adventures emerging in my life and tackle any challenges with purpose and faith in my new journey.

I still live my life one day at a time and at times it is moment by moment depending where I am in my grieving. I remember a song (I know the chorus to a lot of songs that pretty much fit any occasion) and it goes *some days are diamonds; some days are stone.* This pretty much sums up my life. Today, my life is like a diamond. Tomorrow? Who knows.

My passion for writing nudges at the edges of my mind. My creative spirit is stirring. Until now, photography has been my only creative lifeline through grief. Taking photos of my natural world around me is healing and nurturing to my broken spirit and damaged emotions.

People seem to love the photos I take so I keep going. Nature, in the form of wild, untamed seas and windswept cliff tops is my playground and a photographer's dream. Mother Nature makes me smile again as I delve into my passion for her in creative ways.

Writing has been dormant these last months and I am ready to write once more. My inner creative writer has healed enough to put pen to paper (or rather fingers to computer). My personal story through grief is being journaled and it is with clarity and understanding that I see it as a metaphor for other women on their healing journey.

Excitement stirs me into action. I believe in myself and where my journey is taking me.

'*I am worthy*' runs as a rampant thought in my mind. New words, new feelings. I sing out loud, I am worthy, la la la la la, I *am* worthy! I do a little happy dance and keep singing my praises with these three little words.

I have shed twelve kilos. I am fitter and healthier than I have been in a long, long time. I shop for new clothes, a smaller size. I study hard, I love my new home, my family, my friends, my community and my red furry angel. Yippee! Finally I feel good about myself and believe that my inner Goddess is starting to surface from the ashes of my grief.

MEDITATION
Dragon's Breath

Dragon flies low over the highest ridges of the mountains, its fiery breath leaving a smoky trail for me to follow.

I track Dragon over the ridges and deep into the valleys, knowing that my initiation into new and personal healing ways awaits me if I follow the right trails.

My instincts are telling me that this is the right trail to follow.

Three days pass and I follow Dragon's breath every step of the way. I know instinctively that Dragon will lead me directly to my initiation into healing. I just need to trust.

I climb to the top of the next ridge. It is to be the final trail. Dragon swoops down to me, saying, *'You have completed your initiation into new healing ways by using your instincts to follow a trail that had no definitive destination. This is the measure of a true healing woman.'*

'A wounded woman will seek many trails in the pursuit of personal healing. The healing path will only open to her when she trusts her instincts and follows the trails of higher guidance.'

I have been totally absorbed in following the trails to my initiation. I am fully present to my journey toward healing.

In my wisdom, I now recognise that my healing journey had begun the moment I stepped trustingly onto the initial trail of higher guidance.

⌒— AFFIRMATIONS INSPIRED BY MEDITATIONS —⌒

**Follow your own trail/
your intuition is true/
you are a healer/
you have healed yourself/
pursue your dreams/
trust your journey**

Chapter Fourteen

℘ That's what Friends ℘ are For...

November

There is an old feeling buried deep within me called loneliness. It threatens to swamp me at times.

Clearly I have moments of insanity; I think I still miss him. I lurch between wanting his arms around me and a new man's arms to embrace me. Happiness is my companion most of the time, however the underlying feelings of loneliness take their toll and my poor old body is showing signs of wear and tear. I ache from head to toe; I can barely walk or function in a useful way. My body, as my barometer is not happy.

Homeopathics are my saviour as I am brought back to wholeness with remedies and a good talking to by my homeopath. My own programs and meditations are helping me understand old stories that are emerging to be healed.

Recognising that I am lonely for a man's arms around me triggers old beliefs that I need someone to keep me safe. I want a 'backup' if things go horribly wrong. Discovering that I need to love me first is quite a revelation. I have lived my whole life with 'someone', first my family and then my intimate relationships.

Months passed before this reality sinks in; that being on my own is a blessing. Embrace it. I soon realise that I actually like the person I live with—me.

'You look the best you have in years,' a friend tells me. 'You are more serene and beautiful instead of trying to always please him.'

Good friends are so good for my ego. I love it!

In recent years I have been a frumpy, overweight, unhealthy woman. Those who have only known me a short time are amazed at my profound transformation. What they don't realise and what takes time for me to also realise is that I have returned to being the real me; the woman who is usually happy and content, the woman who usually radiates warmth and love, health and vitality.

Overweight, overeating, gorging unhealthy foods, lack of exercise and anxiety had all taken their toll on my self-worth and my health. Changing my circumstances was not an option as I thought I was in love. I was 'in love' with an idea of what I wanted him and our relationship to be.

Recognising my destructive patterns when I have lived for fourteen years in total denial about myself is confronting. When reality tapped me on the shoulder and said *'Hey, look at yourself and how you are destroying something beautiful.'* I buried it with the spade of denial.

Friends and family are wonderful as they support my transformation. I am a butterfly emerging from her cocoon. Five months post EVENT and life is getting easier.

The house I have created as my sanctuary is everything I asked for; my study course brings me immense joy and stimulation. I feel nurtured and safe with all I have created. For the first time in my life, I am truly happy—just with me. I am at peace. I am finding out that I am an okay human being.

My skin is glowing with good health and I have more energy than I have had in many years. I am thirteen kilos lighter thanks to a good eating program and my meditations.

My ego taps me on the shoulder and demands I call him to let him know what he is missing out on. I am not sure what I expect to happen but I want to rub my newfound happiness in his face. Do I think he will suddenly have a change of heart and say he made a mistake and wants to come home?' I wonder how I would respond if that were a reality.

My mind plays several scenarios over and over and nothing would give me greater pleasure than to give a holier-than-thou response: *'Oh no, that door has been firmly shut. I just want to rub your lying face in the ashes of the hurt you caused me,'* or *'Pfft, I have emerged into a Goddess since you left, why would*

I want to relive old hurts?' However a small part of me wonders if I still want him back.

Bugger, I thought this was over.

Do I feel good about bragging to him about how awesome I feel? Actually, yes I do! I need him to know that I am not wallowing in self pity. A good dose of ego tending doesn't go astray at times.

I ask myself, 'Do I feel like a Goddess yet?' Yes, I think I do!

Trying to maintain a friendship with an ex takes effort. People can only be friends if two people put in the effort. It is a sad revelation that we cannot even be friends when I am the only one putting any effort into establishing a new sort of relationship with him.

I have a final hurdle to jump with him. We have a house to sell and it refuses to release me from its materialistic grasp. Our house is now our only connection. Doubt and fear plunge me once again to the depths of grief. Will this never end? It is, in reality, only five months but it feels like lifetimes and I am sick (literally) and exhausted. Let it be over, once and for all. I want him out of my life forever.

He has not contacted me even though he agreed to be friends. I am done with him now. I have grown so much in myself that I want and need so much more for myself. I am finished with him totally.

I don't know if I have the energy to keep moving ahead when there is still a tangible, albeit tenuous, link between us.

Mental and emotional exhaustion take me into a memory of women's business I attended long ago.

A beautiful Aboriginal ceremony on the NSW south coast is where Minmia initiated a hundred women into womanhood. This ceremony had a profound effect on me. At the completion of our initiation, we sat on the beach for four hours in silent reflection. Do you know how difficult it is for a bunch of women to sit in complete silence? Quite a challenge for some. Personally, I loved it. Being at one with our natural surroundings encouraged us to discover what it means to the individual to be a woman. Even then I was obviously pondering the Goddess within!

Dragonflies hovered over me as I sat on the beach, dolphins played just off the shore. I wrote a lot in my journal over those four hours but there was one profound passage that has encouraged me on my journey throughout the years since this ceremony was undertaken.

Have courage to face the journey of your life! Courage to be liked or disliked; success or fail; courage to stand firm in your beliefs and never waver if you know them to be true; courage to admit your mistakes and see things from another's perspective; courage to win and courage to lose; courage to try new things; courage to speak out and to know when to remain silent; courage to just be yourself, warts and all; courage to play by the rules but know when it's okay to break them.

Still in a delightful meditative state, my hand gently brushed a pair of gossamer-winged dragonflies as I left the beach. Minmia told me you only need to look into the eyes of the dragonfly to see the souls of the old women. It was explained to me that the message of Dragonfly is that life will be tough going for a while but it will be resolved. Courage would indeed become my banner of protection.

I recall this women's initiation now as a reminder that I am Woman first and a Goddess in the making. I can take on anything and win as long as I have courage as my guide. Wholeness comes from embracing who I am, not as an extension of someone else. I may have been discarded by the man I professed to love and who professed to love me, but the words, *I am enough* is my new mantra.

MEDITATION
Stand Tall

I wander amongst the wildflowers that grow abundantly in my forest. I stop to admire a new bud, a colourful array, a new shoot.

I bend to touch a withered flower bud sitting in the middle of a thorny bush. As I reach out to remove the bud the bush rises to prick my finger.

My blood falls in droplets to the earth beneath the flower. I look in wonder as it is quickly absorbed into the earth. As it does, the once withered flower begins to bloom into its full magnificent glory.

The flower raises its beautiful head and I can see it growing tall and strong. What was once thought to be withered and dying only needed a gentle touch and a nurturing drop of life giving blood in order for its life force to be returned.

I feel the bloom of my own life force stir within my womb. I had thought my womb barren and withered; no longer able to create beauty as it ages along with my body.

The flower dips its beautiful head and the thorny protective bush moves aside to allow it to touch my womb.

What once lay barren is now once again full of life, beauty, and my creative spirit. I will always bloom in my beauty no matter what the aging process may bring into my life.

⌒ AFFIRMATIONS INSPIRED BY MEDITATIONS ⌒

Live in abundance/
nurture your life-force/
your creative spirit stirs within your womb/
you are beautiful and strong

Chapter Fifteen

❧ Surrender Versus Control ❧

December

'How many times do I need to surrender the sale of our house?' I yell at the Universe. 'As often as needed' is the gentle reply.

I am a master of surrender—for a time. There is a statute of patience on surrender I reason. When something doesn't happen quickly I take back control once more. However, the more I attempt to control the situation the more out-of-control I become. It doesn't seem to matter how much I believe in something with all my heart, my humanness often gets in the way of great manifestation.

Is he lying to me again? Will the sale go my way? Will he keep his promises of equal settlement? These are the thoughts jumping up and down in my head. Anxiety is running rife through my body and I hate it! Most of my goals have fallen into place effortlessly so why are my self-worth issues rising from the ashes to be examined yet again? Am I only worthy of creating small stuff? Do I believe that I am not worthy or capable of creating life's big experiences and adventures?

Realisation stabs me with a red hot poker in my heart. I flinch as the realisation that I don't *feel* worthy of seeding and creating lasting success for myself sinks in. Dropping to the floor because my shaking legs will no longer hold me upright, the intensity of my lack of self worth builds until it grips me like a vice.

I don't know how long I sit there on the cold hard floor but finally, the initial pain wears off and I stagger outside to look at the dark grey clouds building on my horizon. No wonder our house isn't selling; the lesson of worthiness has come knocking on the door of my new life and asked to be let in. An unwelcome guest, but one I must embrace if I am to move through the pain of old patterns. Shaking my fist at the sky, I yell 'I will win you know. I will succeed in my life. You can knock me over and make me feel things I don't want to feel but I WILL win. Watch me!'

Pain and rage recede until I am left with a sense of relief that something has shifted and I know, without a shadow of a doubt that I am growing into my worthy Goddess self.

Now that I am back on a somewhat even keel I make a wish. I want a new, loving partner to come into my life. I am sure I expect someone on a white charger to come in and sweep me off my feet. Fairy tales have a lot to answer for in my book.

Outwardly I am moving forward and getting on with life. Anxiety over the house sale is still prevalent and I am frustrated that I still need to be in contact with him. 'Just get it done,' I rail at the Universe.

I am once again building a shopping list of qualities I would expect in a new partner. What a contradiction I am; frustrated at my ex-partner and his distinct lack of enthusiasm in anything Jude-related and at the same time I want to create and welcome a new partner who embodies anything God-like into my tangled life? I am a bundle of nervous energy. At least I am consistent if a little unbalanced. Not that you will know it outwardly.

My list of qualities that I will accept in a partner is not leaving any room for that something extra special. The limits I place on myself and a future potential partner is restricting the flow of creative energy. Still no one comes knocking on my door! It will be some months before I am ready to leave that choice up to the Universe. Control has become my middle name in the love stakes *and* the house sale.

A tantrum usually clears the air. I scream out loud and stamp my foot, rather petulantly I think. 'Okay, I don't need or want a new partner right now. I surrender,' I declare, but I add a tiny disclaimer, 'for now.' I tell myself 'I'm worthy of great love, but I don't need it in my life right now.'

Healing my old painful wounds must be my first priority. The sanctity of my womanhood has been deeply wounded by betrayal. The man I thought was in love with me walked away from our relationship and left a gaping hole in my heart. Until I heal my wound, I will draw more men to me who will only deepen the pain. What a realisation.

Rousing myself from my warm bed the next morning, I head outside to greet the morning sun. It is a new day, let the healing begin!

MEDITATION
A New Day

The dawn of the new day shines brightly over the water. Golden rays reflect on the floor of the earth at the edge of the sea.

I rouse myself from the deep slumber of the night to witness a new birth. I feel inspired by the huge orb that hangs low in the sky, becoming fully awake as it rises to shine its light upon the world.

I feel my creative spirit stirring deep within my womb. The warmth of the sun and the sound of the waves crashing on the shore are birthing something new and tribal within me.

Contractive pains shift me from my reverie. New waves of light lift me into the highest realms of altered consciousness. The wisdom of the dawn of my new day is birthed through the womb of my wounded woman; light healing the birth canal and the dark recesses of my most secret place within.

I utter a primal cry of new birth and wrap my arms around me; ready to fiercely protect and gently nurture my new-born creation.

ᎧᏋ AFFIRMATIONS INSPIRED BY MEDITATIONS ᏋᎧ

**Birth a new dream/
your inspiration is strong /
embrace your creative spirit/
protect your dreams/
your inner light illuminates the path ahead**

Chapter Sixteen

⌒ Falling into Place ⌒

December

The thought that the house isn't selling is a constant. However, I am more content now and I am sure I have turned a positive corner on life's journey.

Stepping out onto the balcony of my personal sanctuary to take photographs of the most vibrant sunset I have seen in a long time is heart opening. Peace feels like a precious gift at this moment in time. As soon as I step onto my balcony fifty or more dragonflies wing their way past me over a fifteen minute period. Some stop to hover near me, some buzz me on their way past and others are doing loop-the-loop as they all head westward!

My dragonfly messengers let me know in spades that I am through the worst of my grieving. Their sheer numbers tell me that I am moving forward in leaps and bounds and they are lighting the way forward for me.

Dragonflies bring colour and light into my life and encourage me to remove my old rose-tinted glasses. I can see now beyond the illusions that life presents to me. My inner-truth filter has become more discerning in what is right. Their very presence is inspiring.

One of the bigger goals I set for myself in those early days of grief was a trip to New Zealand. As I am currently nowhere near being financially stable, I have no idea how this is going to manifest into my life. The trip is planned for March 2013 and here I am at the end of 2012 with no extra funds. I am just surviving to say the least. All I have is a belief that I am supposed to be a part of this spiritual journey to the North Island of New Zealand. Belief doesn't pay the bills, however all I can do is surrender, sit back and let it unfold naturally.

As the house is still not sold, I fluctuate between belief in the successful creation of my New Zealand goal and taking back control by harassing the real estate agents.

January

I dream I am in New Zealand and this strengthens my belief that I will be there in March. I still have no excess money or a passport and yet I know I am going.

The frustration I feel that this man is still in my life because of the house sale or rather lack of house sale is making me physically sick.

I hate dealing with the agents and I hate that this is not happening quickly. Sure it is still in the right and divine order of my life but time is running out and I need to take charge. I don't even have enough money for a passport yet let alone the ticket! I claw back control of my perceived destiny date with New Zealand.

When I feel on top of my game I believe *all* things are possible even when I can't see tangible proof. The house sale and my trip to New Zealand are the final goals to be achieved in this current round of goal setting.

I am dreaming again; powerful dreams that show me the end of this cycle and that I am packed and ready to step into the new world, my new world. In my dreams my red furry angel is always by my side.

Finally, the rose-tinted glasses are firmly replaced by a deeper inner seeing and knowing about this old relationship.

He treated me badly with his lies, secrets, deceit and belligerence. This went on for years. He seems to think that by staying in our relationship that he tried to make it work but the reality is that he didn't try at all. Nothing ever changed.

Mourning my ideal of what I hoped he would be in relationship with me is still a part of my life. In spite of everything there is a part of me that still misses him and his strong arms around me, but I don't miss the deception. Discovering that I can miss him and yet not want to be with him is a relief. No chance of him coming back anyway.

Questions form in my mind. *Do I feel lonely?* In truth I am not sure. *Do I want a new partner one day?* Yes. *How would I feel to have to consider another person again?* I honestly don't know. I can't imagine being on my own for the rest of my life and yet it terrifies me to think about getting into another intimate relationship. What a contradiction I am in thoughts and feelings.

I moved to the ocean from my mountain home with so much joy and love and hope in my heart. The space I am in now is so different to the one I planned for myself.

Loving myself and doing things that suit just me for a change is a steep learning curve. Life turned me upside down. I grieved deeply the end of my long term relationship and I have come out fighting not only for my survival but the emergence of my inner Goddess.

Gratitude rather than anger fills me. He came here to begin a new life with me and over the course of a few short months he made a decision that our time together was over; our soul contract had expired so to speak. He may not have seen it exactly that way however that is how it has played out. I am grateful for the experience even though it was excruciatingly painful.

Good days outweigh crappy days now and I love my life. I surrender my final goals yet again as my controlling influence is no doubt stopping the flow of the divine order of my life.

The Well has become my confessional, my church, my place of prayer and ritual—my healing place. On my crappy days I yell 'The lies and deceit and secrets were not okay!' and I release the last of my attachment to him. On my good days I say 'Thank you.' I deserve so much better for myself.

One particularly crappy control filled day I yell at the Universe, 'Sell the house, I want done with him NOW!' I demand instant release. I stamp my feet like a child throwing a tantrum because things are seemingly not going my way.

Just as quickly as it appeared, my tantrum is over. 'I'm sorry for yelling!' I say with remorse.

Gratitude fills the lovely empty space left behind by the release of my tantrum. I live in a fabulous house with incredible sunsets, I am part of a loving community, my red furry angel is my constant companion, my study is stimulating, I have shed twenty kilos in weight and I am fitter and healthier than ever before. I am at peace.

My mind hears that the house will be finalised by February 7. I am content with that information. I don't think about the need for a new partner as much now. I am happy to take life as it comes. A new chapter in my life story is just beginning.

I dream of my direction and people lining the streets congratulating me on taking the right road. My friends and family are lovingly supportive of me.

Contacting him to talk about house stuff is no longer a problem. I call him to release money for house bills. Without warning or time to reflect on what I was about to do, I blurt out 'Would you like to keep the house and pay me out?' Where did that come from I wonder. It is effortless from then on as this is what he has wanted to do all along, apparently.

Another dream and I am closing and locking the door on my relationship with him for good. I know now that all is well and moving in the right direction. February 7 arrives and the house settlement is finalised. I am content and so is he. We both get what we need and want.

The key of freedom has just been handed to me—finally. The old mortgage is settled and although there is not much money left, I have enough to get me to New Zealand. Six weeks until I step onto a plane and I still need a passport.

I revel in the fact that although I will achieve my goal, this part of my journey is not so much about material gain as it is about healing my inner wounds. I am finally free of my past. I soar with the freedom of my spirit and the release of old bonds of a life that is no longer relevant to my present and future journey.

MEDITATION
Woman's Strength

The tears that flow, unseen by my husband, are provoked by the same bullying that always came after the lies.

I hide my face lest he see my tears and rise up against me again. I swipe at my tears, a swift movement that is almost defiant in its gesture.

'How did I get to this point?' I wonder. 'How did I allow myself to become a beaten woman?'

I bow my head, breathing quietly, maintaining my dignified silence in the face of my tormentor.

'He tries to break me', I ponder, 'he breaks my body, but he can *never* break my spirit'.

This is what riles him so. What he sees reflected in my own eyes is his ugliness; his ugly vindictive self.

I consider a question I have asked myself over and over. 'Why don't I just leave?' I consider my question for a moment. 'Why is there no simple answer to such a simple question?'

As I stand in that single moment, I hear the call of Mother Earth, my ally, offering up my courage and strength. A subtle change in vibration that I feel deep within the core of my being is all I need to square my shoulders and declare enough is enough.

I catch an imperceptible movement out of the corner of my eye. A hand raised to strike. I stand firm. *This* time I will *not* cower.

My attacker hesitates for a moment in the face of my defiance. Defeat *will not* overcome me this time. I stare him in the eye; his arm still raised, before finally lowering it to his side.

His shoulders slump; my attacker defeated by the strength of my will to live. In that single moment I am transformed and walk away, vowing never to return.

The sun has finally set on my old violent life. I have won and my healing journey has just begun.

Note: Standing strong against bullying by anyone is just one of the messages in this story. This is a metaphoric story about standing strong and walking away from any situation that no longer serves you by encouraging you to find the best solution for you that holds a positive outcome. This includes the violence we hold for self and our personal perceptions about where we are heading in life.

ᖪ— AFFIRMATIONS INSPIRED BY MEDITATIONS —ᖫ

**Embrace your personal power/
you are strong and courageous/
Mother Earth is your friend/
face your fears/
you have won**

Chapter Seventeen

✑ The Last Goodbye ✑

February

He is collecting the last of his belongings on Sunday. This is the final contact and I know it is for the best.

No effort on his part has been made to maintain a friendship anyway, so why would I keep that door open when my dream has very clearly told me this old door is shut and locked.

Looking out my window I watch him walk to my door. My heart skips a beat at the sight of him after all this time.

He steps across the threshold of my sanctuary and I long for him to hug me. I want to feel his arms around me one last time. My own arms lie limply by my side and it takes all my might not to throw them around him in a warm and welcoming embrace. Perhaps I should pack a punch instead and shake off this residual feeling of love?

Why am I doing this to myself? Why am I still not angry at him for all of the lies and secrets? Familiarity is the breeding ground of my own personal deception. My heart is playing tricks, telling me that love still exists in me.

We pack his car and talk one last time. 'I am confused,' I tell him. 'I am not sure if I miss you or just the familiarity of you.' We are comfortable in each other's company as always which is disconcerting after all these months apart.

I say 'I loved you dearly.' He replies with the same reply he always gives, 'I loved you as much as I could love anyone.' It takes four more days after he leaves for the grieving to begin once more. I am wracked by deep painful emotions over the finality of my relationship to this man.

Days pass and my sanity eventually returns. To the outside world I am strong and coping well. It is in my solitude that I unravel and still grieve. Nearly eight months after the EVENT and my friends must be tired of me saying I am still grieving. I remain quiet and grieve in the privacy of my home.

People tell me that there are much worse things happening in the world but I cannot measure my grief by outside events. My grief is *my* grief —I am the only one who can own it.

My passport arrives just one week out from the trip of a lifetime. Nine months have passed and the time is ripe to give birth to my new life. Healing my pain over the preceding nine months was challenging and cleansing. Now I am ready to embrace new adventures.

Every goal I set for myself in the early days of grief has now become manifest in my life. When I step onto that plane, my new life will be birthed.

March

I know there may be relapses but there may not be as well. I will not try to second-guess what my soul has in store for me. What I do know is that right now, I seem to be stepping up and stepping out of the grief.

'You are luminous and glowing with vitality,' my friends tell me. What a wonderful word! Luminous! I must be doing something right. I am not sure I see what they see yet but their words sound good to me.

Compliments have not been a common occurrence in my life. In private I look in the mirror and try to see what they see. Some days when my inner Goddess emerges I get glimpses of it. Understanding is like the proverbial light bulb moment over my head. When I feel good about myself, people respond and notice accordingly. I get it, vibrancy comes from within. Intellectually this is not a new concept, but now I am experiencing it.

My old life is dead. The memories remain but my wound has finally healed.

MEDITATION
Garden of Life and Death

The garden is fragrant with wisteria and jasmine, ginger and roses.

I sit on my overstuffed chair in the centre of my secret garden. Colours and aromas mingle together to beguile my senses. I breathe deeply; breathing aroma and colour alike.

My senses tingle with the bliss I am experiencing.

My mind, my body and my spirit are so tired. Soon, my body will return to the earth. I am very old now and I know my time has almost come.

I sit in my secret garden every day, loving the experience of the warmth of the sun on my aching body, relishing each moment amongst my beloved flowers.

I sigh contentedly, knowing everything is in perfect order. Should today be the day I die, I will embrace death as it comes to take me home. I have achieved everything I set out to do. I have healed old wounds and I am now content to sit in my garden which has been created with so much love.

I lean back in my chair and close my eyes.

I breathe deeply of the aromas once more and in that precious moment, I quietly slip away.

My healing journey is now complete.

Note: this image and story is not only about the physical death we will all experience one day, it is mostly to do with having healed old wounds and dying to your old way of living. You are finding peace within that metaphorical death.

∽— AFFIRMATIONS INSPIRED BY MEDITATIONS —∾

**Celebrate the death of an old story/
love your journey/
be receptive to welcoming a new life chapter/
breathe in the healing aromas of nature**

Chapter Eighteen

❧ Nine Months ❧
– The Birthing of the New Me!

March

New Zealand here I come! I have no idea what is in store for me. Just knowing that I will return home new and refreshed is enough for now.

My car is packed and I am on the road to new adventure. An hour into my journey and I am stationery on the side of the road; angry and bemused by how quickly my life could have changed forever in just a few seconds. I wish I could say that I could see my life flashing before my eyes as I am almost wiped out by a fast moving logging truck that is drifting further and further into my lane. In reality it happens so fast that all I can do is stop my car in the middle of the road and hope he sees me before it's too late. He keeps coming. I pray that he sees me. In those few precious seconds I see that he is distracted and not focusing on the road. My heartfelt prayer lingers in the air as I hold my breath. He looks up and swerves away from me at the last second. Although I am deeply shocked by the near fatality, I am grateful that I am still here to tell the tale.

My journey has begun with a near fatal altercation. It can only get better from here. As I pack my car only a few short hours before, I make a profound personal decision. I choose to fully embrace my inner wild woman and life with all it has to offer. In those few precious moments when the truck is heading toward me I know, without a shadow of a doubt, that I have a choice. I choose to live life to its fullest.

I arrive in New Zealand and I am surrounded by wonderful loving people, all of whom are embracing life in their own unique way. Bonding as a group is immediate. We set out on a two week journey filled with laughter, ceremony, meditation, practical jokes and more laughter. We move collectively and support each other's journey along the way. What a journey! Freedom is my mentor and adventure is my loving partner.

My wild woman emerges often as I dive into the deep crystal clear waters of Lake Taupo and slide screaming unceremoniously down a natural rock slide into the water below. My confidence grows as I embrace my life to its fullest.

Several men enter my life who are honest, loving, affectionate, communicative and spiritual in the name of friendship. Another new experience. I seem to be gathering experiences like notches in a belt.

I quietly observe their interactions with myself and others. Men who like to embrace and talk openly and honestly with me, who willingly share aspects of themselves has me shaking my head in wonder. *'They really do exist!'* I think. I was beginning to think they only lived in fairy tales.

One beautiful man in particular helps me heal the residue of old wounds. He opens his loving heart to guide me and show me the way forward. His name is Daniel.

At 5:30am one morning we walk to the beach beside the lake where the lights of Taupo reflect dancing on the inky surface. The sun is yet to emerge over the peak of the mountain.

Daniel politely asks me to kneel on the cool sand. A strange request at this time of the morning I believe, however I humour him and kneel down. Reaching out his hand, he gently pushes me over. Before I register what he is doing he asks 'How does that makes you feel and what are you going to do about it?' I reply 'I want to hit you and push you over.' He helps me to my knees and pushes me over again. He asks once more, 'How does that makes you feel and what are you going to do about it?' I reply 'I will get back up again.'

Holding out his hand to help me up, I scramble to my feet. He hugs me as he tells me, 'It doesn't matter how many times you get knocked over in relationships, one day, someone will come along who won't knock you down and he will be worthy of your love.' This has a profound effect on me and I see many things in a new light.

I am humbled to have been healed in this way by being open and present to such wonderful masculine energy.

Judy, our group leader who is also a friend, and her partner, Geoff, demonstrate the beauty of a loving relationship. Daniel talks about his love for his children, Jeffree, the songwriter is proud to share his love of his beautiful music. Our elder's son, Patrick, demonstrates his love for his foster child. Our elder, Whaea Kiri, shares with us her love for her family and community. Our youngest member, Laine, is open with us about the love she has for her partner at home in Sydney. All of these remarkable people show me the true beauty of love.

Loving men do exist. There are tactile, communicative, honest, loving, spiritual men in the world. If I am willing, I will indeed find a man who will come into my life and embody all of these delightful qualities.

Diving into the waters of Lake Taupo shows me that I am ready to dive into love when the time is right. There is nothing to fear and I will swim. Diving into the depths of love will be another breathtaking adventure.

When I return to the quiet solitude of my own home, I discover I am happy and content in my own space and with my own company. If a loving man walks into my life one day then that will be a powerful encounter for me to experience. However, I don't need a man in my life to complete me. My life is good and I am content. I am in perfect balance right now!

My inner Goddess is becoming more apparent! I am enough!

MEDITATION
Inner Fire

I am flushed with joy. Heat permeates my entire body, moving deeply within my secret feminine recesses.

As I lay on the soft white sand, the warmth of the sun, as it shines on my naked body, arouses my passion; my inner fire.

I place a hand upon my womb and feel the inner stirrings of new sensual awakenings. I can feel my body, my mind, my spirit, my emotions healing from past hurts, past traumas.

I run my hand down the length of my body, leaving a tingling vibration in its trail.

My breasts firm and I inhale sharply; this intense feeling enveloping my womanliness is deliciously new and exciting.

I stand and stride quickly to the edge of the sandy cliff top. I dive effortlessly into the deep crystal clear ocean below. The cool water is in stark contrast to the warmth of my sandy bed. The impact of my warm body as it pierces the water almost takes my breath away.

I swim deeper and deeper into the cobalt and emerald sea before I return to the shimmering surface.

A tender smile lights my face as fire and water form a climactic fusion between passion and emotional release.

I am healed and ready to love again!

༃— AFFIRMATIONS INSPIRED BY MEDITATIONS —༃

Arouse your passion/
open yourself to new sensual pleasures/
explore your deeply sacred femininity/
be receptive to emotional release and healing

Chapter Nineteen

∾ **Internet Dating** ∾

April

I am healed and ready for action! Do I dare test the waters of relationship? I actually like who I am. Do I want to potentially rock the boat of my calm emotional waters? I have never felt so comfortable in my own skin. I know it is a cliché but it's true.

I feel so good about myself. I decide there may be space in my life for someone special. My terms of course!

My musings are along the lines of *'Do I want a full time relationship or a companion? Perhaps someone who is part time and there when I need them — wink, wink.'*

Oh the arrogance I have developed during my healing time. The queen of control is hard at work as usual. I gather my thoughts and confidently declare *'I want to work with my passions which are my personal development programs and somehow fit a relationship in around my life.'* Hah! I hear a small voice inside of me say *'Be careful what you ask for, because you will get it!'*

There is not a lot of scope for meeting that special someone in the tiny town in which I live. A friend convinces me that I need to go online to the dreaded dating sites. Never in a million years did I dream that I would be one of the many single middle-aged women embarking on an Internet dating (read shopping list here) frenzy. I have rebelled against this in these past months however I am sure I am ready to attempt to navigate the stormy and sometimes treacherous waters that is Internet dating.

I have my (shopping) list of qualities I want in a man so I am ready to begin. Oh my, the fear of getting into a new intimate relationship and sharing my most intimate self with a man terrifies me. My wild woman says, '*Nothing ventured; nothing gained,*' so in I dive, boots and all.

Do people really think about what they write in their profile? Does everyone really mean that they are romantic? I mean to say, if they were romantic, why aren't they still in their relationships? Do they all really want to walk along the beach and still be holding hands when they are old and grey? Do they really want to explore markets/galleries/cafes on weekends and sip lattes by a cosy wood fire? I mean everything I read seems such a cliché and yet here I am professing exactly the same things.

We all want to be loved and would like to think we have love in abundance to offer in return. The truth of the matter is that people are looking for an ideal (I discovered that I am well and truly a part of this group) and yet still have issues of their own to burn!

I decide to 'bite the bullet' so to speak and tentatively add some photos and general information to a couple of dating sites. Wow, the response is overwhelming and in the beginning of my internet dating journey, I am more than a little chuffed.

It really is a meat market. There are men from all sorts of ages, backgrounds, leanings, and ethnicity and almost always their profiles sound as though they are searching for an ideal woman who won't rock their ideal of how they want their world to look.

Well, to be fair, I am searching for my ideal man aren't I? I think I am in control in those first few weeks as I dismiss those I don't deem to be what I am looking for.

Several weeks and a couple of encounters later, I realise that I am no different from the men who are on these dating sites. Trawling for perfection is what we are all doing. Reaching for the highest of high, that one (hopefully) attainable person who fits every set of criteria.

Realising that perfection exists only in our minds is like a kid finding out that Santa Claus isn't real. Ouch! It hurts.

We are ALL flawed in some way or we would not be trawling through the many offers that appeal to our ego—discarding this one for being too old, not good looking enough, not my type, doesn't meet my criteria. You get my drift here. I am picky with good reason. I have been lied to, rejected, hurt and suffered in my grief and I don't want to travel the same path this time.

Arrogantly (again) I forget that everyone else on there has also been lied to, rejected, hurt and suffered in their grief. We are all looking for our ideal mate and we expect to find it by looking through photos and short biographies? Now that really is arrogance.

Hindsight is rearing its wise head again! Thank you, hindsight for your gift of belated wisdom. Clearly you are my friend but could my other friend, 'clarity in the moment' please be more present in my life?

Sighing audibly, I ask myself 'Do I really want to go on 'dates' to see if we 'like' each other and then 'see' where we go from there?' It sounds exhausting and time consuming. In my impatience I just want to find THE ONE and settle down to a good life. We would meet, fall in love and that would be that. Great joy and passion and life would move forward with ease and grace.

Sigh!

Apparently the Universe has a few tests along the way for me first. How could I possibly think I could pass go and head straight into a beautiful relationship without paying the price of an intense learning curve first?

Sigh!

My personal experiences in the dating scene are intense! That's a good word for it: intense.

My initial foray into Internet dating was actually several months prior to this. I dipped my toe into the proverbial waters of Internet dating only to have it nipped by piranhas! So excuse me if I don't really count this as 'dating'. I just chalk it up to necessary experience.

Trawling through several profiles of potentially interesting men throws up some nice photos and a profile that would make your hair curl. It was a passionate and sexy well-worded prose. Oh my, was I naive to the ways of the Internet dating world!

I sent the obligatory 'wink' and was immediately contacted by the man in question. However to 'chat' to him online I needed to pay money. I handed over my hard-earned and limited supply of money to the dating website and a chat was set up.

My hormones (at least that is what I am calling it) couldn't wait to explore his claims of passion and hair curling promises.

A chat box lights up and we begin a dialogue. You know the usual: How are you? Where are you? What do you do? The most innocent and inane of remarks and questions.

As we chat, I note that his poor choice of words is beginning to ring alarm bells. The way he writes is nothing like the poetic profile I was attracted to. 'Did you write your own profile?' I ask him pointedly. I might be a little naive but I am not stupid! 'Of course I wrote it!' he fires back at me.

Gulp! 'So' I counter as nicely as I can, 'You are from a small town called Mintabie in South Australia.'

'I moved with my family from there when I was a baby. I now live in the States' he tells me. 'I am a soldier in Afghanistan. I want to come to Australia and meet you. You are beautiful,' he declares, 'I am looking for someone just like you.'

I bet you are, I think.

By now his mastery of the English language is more and more laboured.

More alarm bells sound but I forge ahead. After all, I have paid my money to chat and this is my first real chat with a man online and I was going to see where it went.

I pose my next question carefully and ask him about something in his profile that I am interested in—his 'so called' paranormal experiences. His response is the equivalent of a blank stare. 'What are you talking about?' he finally replies. I call him on it and his tone (remember that this all on chat) becomes nasty and almost violent in its assault.

I finish the chat immediately. Bile rises in my mouth and I want to throw up. Shaking, I think if this is Internet dating then I want no part in it and I quickly delete my profile. I run to my nearest support friend and lick my newly opened emotional wounds.

It would be months before I can be convinced to try again.

MEDITATION
Cave of the Wounded Woman

I seek solace in the cave at the edge of the ocean. My tormentor is searching the cliff tops for any sign of my presence.

Long ago, I challenged his hold on my life and suffered at his hands for control of my feminine power.

In my retreat, I intuitively know that the cave will offer support and the preservation of my feminine power for all eternity.

I know the tides will ultimately take my physical body but my spiritual presence in these deeply feminine caves, which are representative of all women's wombs, will welcome other women in their time of healing.

My tormentor finds me within the cave just as the tides rush forward to envelope both of us, forever preserving the delicate balance of the feminine and masculine.

The gift from Woman is to offer sanctuary as you journey within your personal inner cave to regroup and heal old wounds—to recover the delicate balance of your *own* feminine and masculine.

ᔿ— AFFIRMATIONS INSPIRED BY MEDITATIONS —ᔾ

**Acknowledge your intuition/
embrace your feminine power/
you are healing/
you are no longer the wounded woman/**

Chapter Twenty

✑— **Deep Breath – I'm Ready** —✑

April

Deep breath Jude, here we go again. Ten months post EVENT and I am ready to dip more toes in the Internet dating waters.

My photos and profile are set and I am ready to take a chance on me— again!

Emails fill my inbox about suitable men who 'match' my profile however none resonate with me and I am still a little gun-shy after the last incident.

One man catches my eye and I send him a wink, he winks back. Wow, he responded. I wasn't expecting that. Now what do I do? A few days pass and I wink again. Back and forward we wink at each other for a few weeks. My credit card does a little dance and I take it from my wallet several times to pay the price to chat but pull back just before the button of purchase is pressed.

Several weeks pass and finally I give in and pay for a chat. Nothing, no response. I have just burned my money! Sigh! Will I never learn?

Just as I surrender the whole online dating idea, I receive a call from the man who has been winking at me. Tracking me down through other search possibilities on the Internet (he didn't want to pay the price to chat) he says he wants to meet me. Rather than see him as a potential stalker, I am flattered that he would go to so much trouble to find me. We chat for ages on the phone as I walk the streets (hmmm doesn't sound so good when I say it like that) and set up our first date. I do a little happy dance in the middle of the street. A date! Jude has a date! A man actually likes what he saw and wants to be seen with me!

Emailing each other many times a day and speaking on the phone awakens something deep within me; something I have not felt in a long, long time. My heart. Oh the pain of an awakening heart is intense after lying tattered and dormant for so long.

Three more kilos disappear from my body as I stress about my awakening heart. The anxiety in me is intense. This is the first man I have dated since the EVENT. I ask myself *'What if he doesn't like what he sees? What if I am too fat, not quite right, too airy-fairy for him? What if I am not intelligent enough? What if I disappoint him in some way?'* My feverish mind is in overdrive and my inner saboteur wants me to run as fast and as far as possible.

Not once do I think *'What if I don't like him?'* Old patterning has surfaced around my worthiness and I am not yet aware of it.

Our emails and chats become bolder with each communication. We tell each other that something magical is happening and we cannot wait to meet in person.

I lunge forward and then in my fear retreat a few paces. *'Hold back'* my panicked heart says. *'Jump straight into a relationship'* my mind replies. *'My heart is healed and I am ready'* I tell myself.

In reality I am being tested. My heart needs a work-out and the only way I will see if it has truly healed is to test the waters within the context of a potential relationship.

We meet in an overcrowded restaurant. The chemistry is immediate. He looks me deep within my eyes and tells me I am beautiful and have amazing eyes. I look into his eyes and see myself reflected there. It is rather like a scene from a romantic comedy of which he is a big fan.

The content of our conversation escapes me. I am so absorbed in the moment that we both actually like what we see that conversation is secondary to my feelings of joy.

There is a lot of hand-holding across the table. It's not easy trying to eat your lunch one handed, make eye contact, talk and still look attractive!

We get up to leave and he opens the door for me. This is new! I haven't had anyone do that for me before. He opens the car door and waits until I am seated inside. He is clearly opening the door to my heart at the same time. He is everything I have asked for in my shopping list of qualities. Everything is perfect and the passion between us is immediate and intense.

Those early days are full of joy and passion. We spend three days together laughing and having fun. After he leaves to go home I intuitively sense a shift in energy. My intuition is telling me that something is not quite right.

Insecurities that I think have been dealt with and released through the grieving process rise to the surface of my supposedly healed wound. Apparently not! Fear grips me like a knife to my heart. I begin to question the validity of his feelings for me already.

The confident woman who has healed so much of her old ways is now a gibbering mess. My heart is opening and I lead with my chin or rather my big mouth through fear of being hurt and want assurances that of course he cannot give in these early days.

The wisdom of hindsight tells me I have been used. Every aspect of our time together was like scenes from romantic comedies. He informs me by email that he cannot see me anymore as he is not over the trauma of his ex-wife leaving him. Rather than falling in a crying heap (which I think would have played out as another romcom scene) I say have a good life. He admits 'I actually want someone who is financially secure with her own home.' Ouch!

As soon as it has begun, it is over. What a learning curve.

The positive to come out of it is that I discover that I am a passionate and sensual woman who has a lot to offer in a relationship (no, not just sex). Once I recognised (and forgave myself) where I have briefly and so spectacularly faltered, I once again become the confident, passionate woman I know is the real me. The stirring of my sensual nature has awakened fresh creativity in new areas of endeavour for me and my mentoring business ideas.

Strike two in the dating game. *'Give it another go'* I hear. Oh why do I do these things to myself I wonder. I am not desperate for a man in my life however I have had a lovely taste of being with someone (even though he was a fraud) and now I want to try it again. My heart is closed now though as I don't want to make the same mistakes.

Third time lucky perhaps? There is a new 'wink' in my inbox. I reply and we make a date to meet for coffee. He sends me a text to tell me how attractive I am and that he is nervously awaiting our date. We have a couple of lovely conversations and texts but my heart remains firmly closed.

When I arrive for our coffee date he is so nervous that I feel we will not go forward in any positive way except perhaps as friends and I tell him so straight up. I have just discovered my confident and passionate wild woman and I can't see how he will fit with this persona. Well, apparently I don't do much for a person's confidence when I shoot them down in flames before giving them a chance. He tells me I am beautiful and have the most amazing eyes (what is it about my eyes I wonder).

I decide to give him a chance as he seems a lovely man even though my heart is firmly shut. There are things about him I really like. He is happy with the outcome and I am content to see where it may lead. I discover he has an intensely passionate side that I quite like, however over the next week I discover that there is not much else that would foster a developing relationship other than sex.

I think to myself *'Is this really what I want for myself, is it enough?'* Taking a chance on potential is my undoing instead of trusting the intuitive red flags that are waving frantically in my face.

My intuition comes out with guns blazing and tells me that he will sleep with his ex-wife. I receive a text the following day to tell me he has just spent the night with his ex! Good luck it says! I am not angry but I see these men are far from worthy of this emerging Goddess!

A few more meetings with some nice men and ultimately I find that we are all the same! We have all been hurt and we are looking for someone to spend the rest of our lives with who won't hurt us, leave us or turn into a version of the people no longer in our lives.

I seem to trigger something in these men that makes them run away. I am real and honest, intuitive and passionate and they don't appear to be able to handle it. Do they want someone who plays their games by their rules or will lie to them about who they truly are? Ouch again! I take responsibility for my part in the journey of my life and it hurts to be so raw and open about my 'wounds'.

I make a critical decision that I will not allow myself to be contained by a man any longer. Collapsing myself into relationships in the past and who I thought the other person wanted me to be is no longer an option. Would they really find me more attractive and want me in their life if I became an extension of them and their life? My real and true passionate nature is consistently replacing the old me. I like it like that, as the song goes.

What is my fatal flaw, I wonder. A girl could get really upset if she didn't see the funny side of Internet dating. Am I any different to these men? Do I really want a full time relationship? Am I really ready for that huge commitment in having another person in my space? Or am I just testing the waters of what I really want and/or need in my life? Could I sustain a relationship that might take up a huge chunk of my time?

I don't know the answer to any of these questions but I sure as heck am having fun finding out! Discovering a side of me that has been always been suppressed has been a potent and intense awakening. I quite like that I now embrace this thing called passion.

I will keep exploring my options and who knows, my prince may come charging through the door or the Internet. He also may not and I have to be okay with that. In reality I need to learn to love myself more first. I have room in my life for someone special and when and if he does come riding along then I will embrace him lovingly with all that I am—but *not* at the expense of the empowered goddess I am becoming.

May

I am enjoying sensual freedom. I just need to be me with all that I am. This is my creative spirit at its best. I am confident with myself now, the most comfortable in my own skin that I have ever experienced; the best I have ever felt. I am free to do whatever I want. Just watch me!

I have learned the hard way the lessons of self worth and trusting my intuition. Rather than wallow in self pity over the choices I have made, I choose to embrace them as 'experiences' I needed to have in order to understand what is not welcome in my life, what is old patterning that needs to be released, and what I will welcome with open arms. My life is a story in progress!

MEDITATION
As Above, So Below

The wind gently sweeps the surface of the water like a lover stroking his true love's hair. I stand on the bank of the lake and watch the birds for a while as they glide seamlessly by, coming to rest on the still surface, barely causing a ripple.

As the sun rises above the horizon, I become entranced by its fluid golden rays as they mirror perfectly in the watery reflection below. The images shine in their perfection of 'as above; so below.'

The hypnotic effect of this scene on me touches a yearning deep within me. Placing my hands upon my womb, I yearn to know the pleasure of creating a place in my life for my one true love.

I sink to my knees at the edge of the lake. I lean forward ever so slightly to peer into the water.

I move a little until I can clearly see my reflection on the surface of the water. Like the sun, my image is a clear mirror of myself.

I whisper, 'Show me my one true love'. My reflection does not move.

I whisper my request one more time. This time, my reflection speaks to me and says, *'You are looking at your one true love. I am the very reflection of you. Accepting and loving yourself is the first rule of true love. To create a loving partnership with another in your life you must first accept the love of self for self. It is in this personal acceptance that you create space for another to enter your life.'*

I draw back from the water's edge and accept that my reflection is right. I touch my womb once more and feel an inner shift as a sacred space is created within me. I lean forward once more and smile lovingly back at my own reflection.

࿔ AFFIRMATIONS INSPIRED BY MEDITATIONS ࿔

Truly 'see' your reflection/
recognise the yearning to know true love/
surrender and learn to love yourself/
you are your own true love first

Chapter Twenty-One

☙ Goddess is in the Building ☙

June

It is one year ago today that you walked out of my life. You broke my heart but you didn't break my spirit and I have grown into a stronger and more vibrant version of myself for the experience. What a year! I wouldn't change it for anything!

One year that has taken me on an incredible journey 'From Grief to Goddess'. I have released twenty three kilos from my frame and another seventy two kilos from my life and I feel wonderful. Where did the seventy two kilos come from you may ask? My ex-partner of course.

Finally freeing myself from the burden of loving him through the early months of my healing journey into grief is a relief.

I feel liberated from the confines of a destructive relationship. For the first time in my life I am happy with just me! In twelve months I plunged to the depths of my grief and emerged victorious as my own Goddess.

I research the meaning of the word Goddess and I come across a plethora of meanings. I struggle with dictionary meanings; such as 'one of great beauty or grace' or 'one with supernatural powers' (not that this wouldn't be handy) or 'someone adored especially by men' (now that really would come in handy – perhaps with the supernatural powers).

The reality is that when I researched the meanings of the word Goddess, my old feelings of unworthiness surfaced. I didn't 'feel' worthy of any of the meanings. I felt my old insecurities erupt like an annoying pimple on the face of my worthiness.

Does this mean I have not really moved into my Goddess form? Has my journey through the past twelve months all been a lie perpetuated by my own musings throughout my healing journey from the grief of my partner leaving me?

I am plunged into self doubt over these feelings of unworthiness. Am I really that shallow that my journey is to be undone by a simple word—Goddess?

I throw the dictionary out the proverbial window with its general meanings and sit with what the word, the definition of what Goddess means to me personally.

GODDESS: JUDE'S PERSPECTIVE

A woman who has healed the greater part of her grief, who is deeply immersed in her Divinely Feminine path in life, who has discovered that she actually likes herself a great deal; a woman who has defined her life purpose and uncovered her inner diamond, her worth as a woman, and as a human being.

A woman who has a lot to offer in her world, who is happy in her own company, who can make her own decisions and choices in life and live with the consequences—regardless of what they are.

A woman who is confident and comfortable in her own skin, who glows with vitality and good health, who is responsible and caring, who is never afraid to show love and courage in the face of adversity.

A woman who is willing to show her flaws as well as her strengths, who can laugh at herself and life in general. A woman who can cry openly when she is hurting and ask for help and support when she needs it and is there to offer help and support when others need her.

My inner Goddess embraces all of these qualities and more that I am yet to discover. When I fall down, I pick myself up. When I am happy, I share my happiness with others. The Goddess journey is one of wonder and excitement, pain and hurt and it is the self-discoveries I make along my path that will keep me moving in a positive, forward direction.

This Goddess is ready and willing to take the next step in her life, whatever that may be. This is *my* personal definition of Goddess.

I guess the word Goddess defies one definition. It is who we know we are on the inside and this directly reflects into our external world.

It doesn't matter whether you grieve as male or female. The process is still a painful one and the end result is the healing you have undergone within you with each step along the way. It will take as long as it takes, so be gentle and nurturing of self. You are worthy of great love and a great life.

I know in my humanness that my grief will rise again from time to time however the waves of grief will become less as I take positive steps forward. You don't stop loving someone just because they are no longer in your life. The grieving process is a time of learning about self and what self is capable of and that involves growing into your innate Goddess self.

When the rug is pulled out from beneath us, we find that a new and exciting beginning awaits us once we sift through the ashes of our grief.

Forgiveness is a part of the journey. Forgiving self for the times we fall over and have to pick ourselves up again and again. My journey will continue on from this point in healing my grief and there may still be times when I fall down, again, but I am strong. I am my own unique goddess self and I will survive—always. I will thrive—always. Just watch me!

Goddess is in the building!

MEDITATION
Weaver of Life

Spider sits in the centre of her silken web and watches as I approach.

I walk across the sand, watching for the messages I know will come to me today. All of my senses are alert. My dreams the previous night were filled with intricate spider webs spun into labyrinths indicating impending change.

I know that to dream of spider webs is indeed fortuitous and the message is clear that I will soon be weaving a new web in my life.

I spy the web hanging precariously between the rocks, knowing it is tough and can withstand most events. It is dripping with jewel-like raindrops from the recent shower of rain; vibrant colour reflecting in each drop.

Spider steps forward and introduces herself as a web weaver; a sister to me.

Spider speaks *'It is time for your new web to be spun. Spin only one silk strand at a time. Do not rush the spinning of your web and it will stand up to the tests of time. You will be challenged on this new journey but you are strong and have healed the deepest, most painful stories that resided within you. Your pristine web will take you on exciting new adventures. This is my message to you.'*

I feel the new web beginning to take form. Through my dreams I will shape shift into Spider to weave my web. My dreams will ensure this journey will be taken through to completion. My new life has now begun.

❧ AFFIRMATIONS INSPIRED BY MEDITATIONS ❧

Be receptive to incoming messages/
listen to the wisdom of nature/
harness the power of your dreams/
weave a new life web/
welcome new adventures

❧ **The Stories** ❧

The *From Grief to Goddess* stories or meditations have been created as a powerful healing tool. Each meditative story is a metaphor for life's healing journey.

It is important to remember that to heal the Wounded Woman is an inner journey. When you choose one of the *From Grief to Goddess* meditative stories, you have asked for one of your own personal stories to be healed.

The short stories or meditations at the end of each chapter take you on a journey deep within you to the welcoming and nurturing vibrations of Woman, nature and her healing ways to ultimately awaken your innate inner Goddess. Healing can begin from the moment you choose the story that calls to you.

Working with the *From Grief to Goddess* Healing Cards will add an extra dimension to your healing journey. The image on the cards is a vortex of healing energy drawing you deep within your soul for the purpose of healing one of your personal stories. Each card holds healing affirmations that reflect your bigger story.

Who *is* the wounded woman? She is *all* women who have been persecuted, misunderstood, tortured, belittled and betrayed throughout history by a patriarchal rule. This same patriarchy has raped and pillaged our mother, our home, our earth in the name of power. Woman has also been persecuted by her own kind in the name of fear. There are no boundaries in the realm of healing. Just healing!

Our world has been out of balance for too long. We must bring unequivocal balance to the masculine and feminine, both within ourselves and to our planet. There must once again be equality. We must stop the systematic destruction of our natural world. Masculine and feminine *can* live in perfect harmony. They *must* walk the road of life side by side.

To begin, we must heal the wounded woman within and thus heal our wounded Mother Earth.

Our stories are held deep within our womb. Stories that have been perpetuated throughout history *must* be healed in order to create the life we want to live, in order to have a life to live.

As Woman connects with the inner recesses of her own womb, she will understand the personal story wanting to surface to be healed.

Our journey into healing should be uncomplicated and simple in its approach. I have created these *From Grief to Goddess* stories and Healing Cards as a simple and vibrant healing tool. Storytelling through the art of imagination creates powerful healing for both you and our Mother Earth.

When we are disconnected from our mother, we hurt; our mother hurts. When she recognises the powerful healing taking place within the womb of one of her daughters, she feels the connection instantly and deeply. Our mother will always recognise us. When we heal, she heals. Simple!

Your journey into the healing image and stories will evoke new insights into the personal story needing to be healed within you. Sometimes, the insights may be clear and instant. Other times they will appear in dreams or visions, often when you least expect them. Sometimes your insights will appear in the form of symbols, or animal messengers, a book or a message through a friend or stranger. You do not need to push for insights, they will happen for you at the right time and when they are truly needed. Your insights, as they relate to the healing process, will always be simple! Life is only as complicated as you like to make it!

❧ Introduction to the Stories ❧

Life has taken us on many journeys as we seek wholeness within our life. We have worked long and hard through many years of challenges with relentless and intense work on ourselves. We journeyed inward again and again to heal aspects of a self that felt broken by the many challenges life threw at us.

We clawed our way through, we waded through mire and we often despaired at ever achieving the goals and dreams we had long held close to our heart.

With these intense healing journeys we now have a measure of personal and structural success. We can create anything we want now. We *are* the creators of our new destiny.

To keep the flow of success moving forward in our lives, we must continue to clear away the debris of our inner wounded woman.

This creates a sacred space within us, which is the healed womb of creation. The seeds of new goals and dreams can then be firmly planted and nurtured in this healed sacred inner space.

From Grief to Goddess was inspired by my natural surroundings. It is the culmination of my passions, blended with the simple messages that nature evokes.

The short metaphoric stories and accompanying healing cards will evoke an internal response from you as you heal a personal story erupting within you right now. The healing meditations in the *From Grief to Goddess* book may be worked with on their own, as can the *From Grief to Goddess* Healing Cards. However, by working with both, the healing can be deeper and more profound.

Allow the feelings that working with the meditations and cards evokes to rise to the surface of your consciousness. Your responses may be feelings of love, joy, fear, anger or frustration, passion or whatever comes up for you.

Congratulations on being ready to heal the next layers of your old chapters that are your old wounds!

IMAGINATION IS A POWERFUL TOOL

From Grief to Goddess is an inner journey where you will work with your imagination to heal your inner wounded woman.

Your imagination taps into the infinite possibilities of creation through the power of the mind. You may work with the meditations on their own or you may also choose to work with the healing cards as well.

Your mind can create the mental imagery from the *From Grief to Goddess* meditations and encourage deep inner healing through this metaphoric journey. The added bonus of working with the *From Grief to Goddess* Healing Cards as well, encourages you to journey within the vortex of healing energy illustrated on the cards, to your own inner realms of healing and your inner Goddess. All healing begins from deep within your soul.

WORKING WITH THE MEDITATIONS

The *From Grief to Goddess* meditations are designed to stand on their own merit however to work with them in conjunction with the *From Grief to Goddess* Healing Cards offers an even deeper healing journey.

To work with the metaphoric stories in *From Grief to Goddess* you may like to find your own 'power place' in nature and connect with Mother Earth. You *are* Woman, you *are* Goddess and Mother Earth recognises you as her daughter; a woman undertaking a powerful and profound healing journey!

If you cannot get out into nature, find your own inner sanctuary where you will not be disturbed. It may be a special room or even your own bedroom, wherever feels right to you. You may choose to light a candle and burn incense or vaporise a favourite essential oil. If you choose to be outside, you may like a cushion to sit on, a tree to lean against or to cover yourself with a blanket. Make your space a safe, comforting, loving space.

As you sit quietly in your sacred space, first imagine yourself sitting in a golden bubble of loving, nurturing, protective light. Feel or sense its golden warmth enveloping you like a comforting blanket.

Take a few deep breaths and focus on your intent for healing. Hold the *From Grief to Goddess* book loosely in your hands as you quietly ask for guidance from your soul for your healing journey.

Now hold the *From Grief to Goddess* book against your womb for a few moments. It doesn't matter if you have a physical womb or not. It is the energetic womb with which you are working. This is the place of healing your Wounded Woman and connecting with your innate Goddess self. You are setting your clear intention to heal your attachment to an old story.

Feel your personal story that needs to be healed bubble to the surface of your consciousness. This may be a story that you are already aware of or it may be another personal story that has decided needs healing first. Trust the healing process. It is soul directed.

If you do not know exactly which story needs healing right now, it doesn't matter. Just ask your inner Goddess to show you which story in the *From Grief to Goddess* book will assist you with your inner healing. You don't have to be fixed on the details of the story rising to the surface to be healed.

Once you have quietly asked for guidance in choosing the meditation that is the right one for you right now, open *From Grief to Goddess* and scan the list of meditations in the contents page and 'see' or 'feel' or 'know' which story is more vibrant than the others. Another way is to work with a pendulum to find which meditation is the most important one for you right now.

Whichever way you choose your healing story in *From Grief to Goddess* is the right way for you. You are soul guided to the right one.

Read the meditative story three times, each time absorbing the healing words into your womb to heal the old stories. These are metaphoric stories that you have chosen intuitively.

You *are* Woman! This is *your* healing journey.

Rest the *From Grief to Goddess* book against you or in your lap.

Take three slow deep breaths, in through your nose and release them with a sigh. Take each breath deep into your body. Allow your body to begin to relax. Feel your breath become slow and steady.

Keep your focus on your chosen meditative story as you breathe in relaxing, loving, nurturing, protective energy. Breathe the story into your body. Feel your body becoming heavy with relaxing energy. As you breathe out, imagine you are exhaling anything that is unwanted, unneeded and unhealthy.

Feel your mind begin to relax. Allow your thoughts to ebb and flow effortlessly. Focus on the story and allow your thoughts to slowly fade into the background.

Take a few moments to really immerse yourself into the healing words of the story. Take your focus deep within you to a place of peace and stillness.

Feel Woman's story as yours. Feel the healing energy captured within the words of the story. Imagine yourself merging with Woman, feeling your deeply and Divinely Feminine womanhood. You are courageous, strong and powerful in your personal healing. You are Woman; you are Goddess.

Now that you are relaxed and focussed on the image, take another breath. As you do, you begin to hear the sounds held within the story you have chosen. You may hear the sounds of the ocean as the waves crash onto the shore, or the rustle of leaves in the treetops, or the footfalls of Woman on the soft earth.

As you breathe out, release your attachment to your old story. There are aspects of your old story that are no longer needed. It is time to release its energetic hold on you. Imagine this facet of your story being lovingly released by Woman, your inner Goddess through the healing words.

Breathing in again, you notice you are breathing in the aromas held in the story: an ocean breeze or a damp dense forest or maybe the earth after rain. Breathing deeply into the healing words, you are transported further into this place for the purpose of inner healing.

As you breathe out, release any doubt and fear about your healing journey. Immerse yourself in this healing experience.

Allow your breath to absorb positive healing experiences and release the negative vibration of your old story. You are creating an inspired inner sanctuary with your breath and your journey within.

As you breathe in again, you feel the sensations held within the story; the red earth between your bare toes, or the cool drops of rain on your skin, or the warmth of the rising sun.

As you breathe out, you surrender yourself to your healing. Your body and mind are relaxed and you are fully immersed in this inner healing journey. You have journeyed to this safe, nurturing place within the story.

This is an inner journey where you can and will experience exactly what you need at any given time. This is a positive journey toward healing.

Your breath is slow and steady. You are relaxed. You *are* Woman; you *are* Goddess. This is *your* healing time.

You hear or sense your Goddess messages of healing as you experience this sacred place.

Stay with the healing story for as long as you feel connected. Once this healing session is over, you will feel the energy of your meditation begin to disperse.

Hold gratitude for this journey as you return to your present time and place, bringing with you your feelings of wholeness and healing and your beautiful connection with your inner Goddess firmly in place within you and around you. You *are* Goddess! Take a deep breath and stretch your body. Welcome back!

This healing session is one of peace and transition. You have created an inner sacred space that can now be filled with new ideas and goals as you move into a new way of living your life in powerful and positive ways.

Prior to healing another personal story, give yourself the gift of time before you journey into them again. You need to give your body, mind, soul and emotions a chance to let the healing energies complete their work.

You only heal one story at a time. Work with the personal story presenting itself now until another story bubbles up to the surface to be healed.

Our lives are always a work in progress. Trust your inner Goddess to help you know when each aspect of your story is ready to be healed, these are the stories within the greater story of your life!

For an even deeper healing journey you may also like to work with *From Grief to Goddess* Healing Cards.

WORKING WITH THE MEDITATIONS *AND* THE HEALING CARDS.

Take a few deep breaths and focus on your intent for healing. Hold the *From Grief to Goddess book* and your *From Grief to Goddess* – Healing Cards loosely in your hands as you quietly ask for guidance from your soul for your healing journey.

Now hold the book and cards against your womb for a few moments. It doesn't matter if you have a physical womb or not. It is the energetic womb with which you are working. This is the place of healing your Wounded Woman and connecting with your innate Goddess self.

Feel your personal story that needs to be healed bubble to the surface of your consciousness. This may be a story that you are already aware of or it may be another personal story that has decided it needs healing first. Trust the healing process. It is soul directed.

If you do not know exactly which story needs healing right now, it doesn't matter. Just ask your inner Goddess to show you which story in the *From Grief to Goddess* book and Healing Cards will assist you with your inner healing. You don't have to be fixed on the details of the story rising to the surface to be healed.

Take a deep breath and shuffle the cards until you feel ready to intuitively choose one. You may choose to look through each of the cards and 'see' or 'feel' or 'know' which one feels right to you. One may appear more vibrant than the others. Or, fan the cards out on the table and run your hand slightly above each of them. You may experience a sense of cool or warmth or a tingling sensation in your hand. The card you choose will be an intuitive response to the personal story you need to heal at this moment.

Whichever way you choose your healing card is the right way for you. You are soul guided to the right one.

The *From Grief to Goddess* Healing Cards have healing affirmations as well as the number of the meditative story associated with it. You will find the stories, as chosen by you, in *From Grief to Goddess*.

Take three slow deep breaths, in through your nose and release them with a sigh. Take each breath deep into your body. Allow your body to begin to relax. Feel your breath become slow and steady.

Keep your focus on the image of your chosen card as you breathe in relaxing, loving, nurturing, protective energy. Focus on your affirmation and breathe it into your body. Feel your body becoming heavy with relaxing energy. As you breathe out, imagine you are exhaling anything that is unwanted, unneeded, and unhealthy.

Feel your mind begin to relax. Allow your thoughts to ebb and flow effortlessly. Focus on the image and allow them to slowly fade into the background.

Take a few moments to really immerse yourself into the healing image.

Hold your chosen healing card in your hand and make sure you can see the image clearly. Read aloud the healing affirmations on the card. This healing image, healing affirmations and the corresponding story are the ones you need to focus on right now. Gaze into the vortex image for a moment or two, allowing it to draw your focus inward.

Read the corresponding story from the *From Grief to Goddess* book. You may choose to read it several times to feel and absorb its relevant and healing message. You *are* the woman in this story. You are healing an old story within you.

Feel this story as yours. Feel the healing energy captured within the words of the story. Feel your deeply and Divinely Feminine womanhood. You are courageous, strong and powerful in your personal healing. You are woman; you are Goddess.

Now that you have read and absorbed this story within you, take your focus back to the image and healing affirmations.

The image on the card is designed to draw you into the centre balance point, the axis mundi, to draw you within the mysteries of your soul for deeper healing.

Everything around you becomes a part of your journey—the sounds, the aromas, and your environment.

The more you focus on the image in the card, the more your external stimuli will begin to melt away from your consciousness. The image encourages you to focus on your meditative journey.

Working with your imagination awakens different realms of possibility within you.

Say your healing affirmations a further three times and feel, see or sense your heart and soul opening up to the realms of healing your attachment to old personal stories.

As you gaze into the image of your chosen card, focus on the central balance point of the image and imagine your inner Goddess reaching out her hand to you to take you on a journey within the depths of your soul for the purpose of fostering healing and wholeness.

The metaphoric story or meditation, the colours of the image, the healing affirmations and your inner Goddess are all working to assist you in healing this old story.

Now that you are relaxed and focussing on the image, take another breath. As you do, you begin to hear the sounds held within the image. The sounds associated with the metaphoric story you have chosen. You may hear the sounds of the ocean as the waves crash onto the shore, or the rustle of leaves in the treetops, or footfalls on the soft earth.

As you breathe out, release your attachment to your old story. There are aspects of your old story that are no longer needed. It is time to release its energetic hold on you. Imagine this facet of your story being lovingly released by your inner Goddess through the healing image and story.

Breathing in again, you notice you are breathing in the aromas held in the image: an ocean breeze, or a damp dense forest, or maybe the earth after rain. Breathing deeply into the image, you are transported further into this place for the purpose of inner healing.

As you breathe out, release any doubt and fear about your healing journey. Immerse yourself in this healing experience.

Allow your breath to absorb positive healing experiences and release the negative vibration of your old story. You are creating an inspired inner sanctuary with your breath and your journey within.

As you breathe in again, you feel the sensations held within the image: the red earth between your bare toes, or the cool drops of rain on your skin, or the warmth of the rising sun.

As you breathe out, surrender yourself to your healing. Your body and mind are relaxed and you are fully immersed in this inner healing journey. You have journeyed to this safe, nurturing place within the image.

This is an inner journey where you can and will experience exactly what you need at any given time. This is a positive journey toward healing.

Your breath is slow and steady. You are relaxed. You *are* Woman; you *are* Goddess. This is *your* healing time.

You feel or sense the healing embrace of nature around you. You hear or sense her messages of healing as you experience this sacred place.

Stay with the healing image and the story for as long as you feel connected. Once this healing session is over, you will feel the energy of your meditation begin to disperse.

Hold gratitude for this journey as you return to your present time and place, bringing with you your feelings of wholeness and healing and your beautiful connection with your inner Goddess firmly in place within you and around you. You *are* Goddess! Take a deep breath and stretch your body. Welcome back!

This healing session is one of peace and transition. You have created an inner sacred space that can now be filled with new ideas and goals as you move into a new way of living your life in powerful and positive ways.

When you feel you require a new journey into the healing images and stories, give yourself the gift of time before you journey into them again. You need to give your body, mind, soul and emotions a chance to let the healing energies complete their work.

You only heal one story at a time. Work with the personal story presenting itself now until another story bubbles up to the surface to be healed.

Our lives are always a work in progress. Trust your inner Goddess to help you know when each aspect of your story is ready to be healed. These are the stories within the greater story of your life!

DISRUPTION:

Temporary disruption may be a factor on your healing journey. You have taken positive steps to heal another personal story and the next chapter of your life is now ready to be written.

When you ask for change on life's journey, you need to be ready to move out of your comfort zone. Your soul knows when the time is right to heal the old story and gently nudges you and, at times, unceremoniously pushes you into taking action. It is asking you to make space in your life for your next adventure.

INTEGRATION:

Energetically you have healed and surrendered the old way of living a personal story. Sometimes, in your everyday physical environment, this old story may attempt to hold you to your old way of being. Some people may not understand or respond positively to the new healed you. Situations may demand you return to the old, outworn story. Life circumstances may attempt to undermine this powerful healing journey.

This is a time of integration for you. This is where you integrate your *new* story into your everyday life—step by step. You are filling the sacred space left by the healed old story, with powerful and positive new experiences, goals, dreams and beginnings. There will ultimately be no room in your life for the old story as you make your way forward.

Be gentle with yourself and others as you integrate your very new story into your everyday life. There is no need to rush the journey.

When you re-enter your everyday life with exciting new messages and steps to take in your new story, you may find yourself busy with your everyday life.

The people around you in your family unit and friends and co workers may not want you to step up and move into a new story. They may be comfortable with you as you were when you were living with your old story.

It is up to you to integrate your new steps into your life and maintain your powerful new way of being. Being firm with people and saying 'no' when something is not of greater benefit to your new story will upset some people.

When this happens ask yourself a question: Do I want to undo the healing of my old story so that my loved ones will be comfortable with me again, or, do I want to begin to live my life in the way that serves *me* best?

When you live your best life possible and keep moving forward, sometimes in small increments and sometimes in giant leaps, you will find that people and events begin to change in your life. It is the pebble in the pond ripple effect.

Some people may leave your life and new ones will enter. Some people will grow with you and move forward with you into your new chapter. They are also integrating the new you into their own stories. The key for you is to trust your inner positive guidance that will help you navigate your new story to get the very best out of life.

Life will be filled with challenges along the way but you know how to heal them now and how to work with them to learn and grow from them. This is all part of your life story.

Be gentle with yourself and others as you continue to write and rewrite the chapters of your life. It is an exciting journey!

DESIGN AND CREATE YOUR NEW STORY OR CHAPTER

Each time you heal an old personal story, you create more and more light-filled space within you in which to design and create the life of your dreams.

It is time to design the life you really want for yourself. These are the very first chapters of your new story, which is part of the greater story of your life. Each new chapter will describe the flow of your new story, welcome new characters and say goodbye to some of the old ones. You will set new scenes and have new adventures and also some new challenges along the way.

You are the designer and the creator of your life, your new story.

You have cleared away the old debris and you are ready to create new foundations.

Take a walk in nature. Walk amongst the trees; sit by a river or ocean.

Get up at dawn and watch the sunrise. Nature is your inspirational guide.

With your imagination, begin to design the life you want for yourself. Be detailed, see vivid images or have a sense of them.

Once you have designed this new story and know how you want it to look, it is time to begin creating it.

- Find your quiet place and take a few deep breaths. Take your focus inward and ask your inner Goddess for the first few steps, your personal insights as you journey toward the creation of your new story.
- Keep a journal and record your dreams, visions, and inspirations.
- Take only the steps you are intuitively given. To push any further ahead than your guidance is willing to share with you will only create obstruction in your life.
- There is no set time to creating this new story. It is about following your inner guidance each step of the way until this particular story is fulfilled.

Remember that our personal stories are always a work in progress. There will be many re-writes along the way!

Heal the old story, design your new story, and take the first vital steps of new creation to live the life of your dreams.

Acknowledgments

The loving and unconditional support of my beautiful family and friends was an important part of my healing journey and in the writing of this book. It is humbling to know that I am so well loved and supported in my life.

I want to thank my sons Adam and Tim and my gorgeous granddaughters Keira and Lacey for being the most glorious young people I know. I am a lucky Mum and Gran.

Thank you to my Mum for worrying about me and being there when I needed her.

To my beautiful friends, thank you for always being the supportive network I needed throughout this journey and beyond. A special thank you to Tina, Birdy, Dot, Debbie, Julia, Angie, Kathy, Victoria, Anne, Kellie, Nicole and Bobbie for listening and offering your unconditional support and hugs.

An extra special thank you to Angie Alexandrou for allowing me to use her beautiful artwork for the *From Grief to Goddess* book cover and the Healing Cards.

A huge thank you to the very special community in the South West of Victoria who adopted me and supported me throughout this journey. And a special thank you to the wonderful people I travelled with in New Zealand, Judy, Geoff, Daniel, Kiri and Laine. What a healing journey!

I wish I could name everyone who has played an important part on my journey but there are so many that it would be a book in itself! You are in my life, thank you.

A big thank you to Scott and Trudy King from Animal Dreaming Publishing for believing in me and supporting me every step of the way in this publishing process. You are not only my publishers but my dear friends as well! What a learning curve it has been! Thank you one and all; simply thank you for always 'being there' for me.

Also by Jude Garrecht

From Grief to Goddess Healing Cards

21 HEALING CARDS
WITH INSTRUCTIONS FOR USE

Your inner Goddess reaches out from deep within the vortex to take you on a healing journey as you meditate on the affirmations and powerful artwork.

The 'From Grief to Goddess Healing Cards' are an effective tool to encourage the release and deep inner healing of old personal stories. Are you ready to write the next chapter in your life story?

www.fromgrieftogoddess.com